English as an Additional Language

English as an Additional Language

Approaches to Teaching Linguistic Minority Students

Edited by
Constant Leung and Angela Creese

Los Angeles | London | New Delhi
Singapore | Washington DC

SAGE Publications Ltd
1 Oliver's Yard
55 City Road
London EC1Y 1SP

SAGE Publications Inc.
2455 Teller Road
Thousand Oaks, California 91320

SAGE Publications India Pvt Ltd
B 1/I 1 Mohan Cooperative Industrial Area
Mathura Road
New Delhi 110 044

SAGE Publications Asia-Pacific Pte Ltd
33 Pekin Street #02-01
Far East Square
Singapore 048763

Library of Congress Control Number: 2009931134

British Library Cataloguing in Publication data

A catalogue record for this book is available from the British Library

ISBN 978-1-84787-531-0
ISBN 978-1-84787-532-7 (pbk)

Typeset by C&M Digitals Pvt Ltd, Chennai, India
Printed in Great Britain by CPI Antony Rowe, Chippenham, Wiltshire
Printed on paper from sustainable resources

Contents

List of tables

Appendix

Contributors

Kimberly Cook is an Adult Education ESL teacher for the Alachua County School District in Gainesville, Florida. She has been teaching ESL for the past 19 years. She has been an ESL teacher-educator for Saint Leo University and for K-12 teachers in the local school district, and she regularly supervises preservice teachers in their ESL teaching practicum at the University of Florida. She has a Master's degree in Multilingual/Multicultural Education from the University of Florida.

Angela Creese is Professor of Educational Linguistics at the School of Education, University of Birmingham. Her research focuses on interaction in multilingual classrooms. Her work is theoretically and methodologically informed by anthropological linguistics and she has used this approach to investigate teacher collaboration in linguistically diverse schools and bilingual interaction in complementary and mainstream schools.

Rebecca Freeman Field has conducted ethnographic/discourse analytic research on bilingualism and education in multilingual communities, and consulted with schools on language education policy, program and professional development. Her books, *Bilingual Education and Social Change* (1998), *Building on Community Bilingualism* (2004), and *English Language Learners at School: A Guide for Administrators* (2006, co-edited with Else Hamayan) promote equal access to educational opportunities and multilingualism through schooling. She is currently Adjunct Professor at the University of Pennsylvania and Director of the Language Education Division of Caslon.

Candace Harper is an Associate Professor in ESL/Bilingual Education at the University of Florida. She has been an ESL/EFL teacher and teacher-educator in the USA, Australia, Bosnia and France. Her research interests have focused on language and literacy development in EAL learners, the nature of EAL specialist teacher expertise, and the preparation of general educators to work effectively with EAL learners. She is currently studying the collaboration of ESL/bilingual and other curriculum specialist educators.

Margaret R. Hawkins in an Associate Professor in the Department of Curriculum and Instruction at the University of Wisconsin-Madison. Her research focuses on languages and literacies of English learners in schools, community-based sites of learning for immigrant and refugee youth, home/school relations, language teacher education, and, most recently, on non-gateway districts' and schools' responses to new immigrant and refugee populations.

Carol K. James teaches at Talbot Elementary in Gainesville, Florida. She has been teaching for 25 years; with EAL students in her mainstream classroom for the past 21 years. Carol is also an ESOL teacher educator for inservice and preservice teachers in Florida. She has a Master's degree in Multilingual/Multicultural Education from the University of Florida, is Reading endorsed, ESOL endorsed, and certified in English as a New Language by the National Board of Professional Teaching Standards.

Ester J. de Jong, EdD obtained her Master's degree from the University of Tilburg, the Netherlands. After receiving her doctoral degree in Bilingual Education at Boston University, she worked for five years as Assistant Director for Bilingual/English as a Second Language programs in Massachusetts. She is currently Associate Professor in ESOL/Bilingual Education at the University of Florida, Gainesville. Her research interests include two-way immersion and other integrated bilingual education approaches, language policy, and mainstream teacher preparation for English language learners.

Constant Leung is Professor of Educational Linguistics at King's College London. He is Director of the MA English Language Teaching and Applied Linguistics and MA Assessment in Education programmes in the Department of Education and Professional Studies. His research interests include education in ethnically and linguistically diverse societies, second/additional language curriculum development, language assessment, language policy and teacher professional development. He has written and published widely on issues related to ethnic minority education, additional/second language curriculum, and language assessment nationally and internationally.

Frank Monaghan is a Senior Lecturer at the Open University. Before joining the OU in 2003 he was a teacher of English as an additional language for 20 years in a large multilingual comprehensive school in central London. His main research interest is in EAL and mathematics, on which he has published a number of articles and led professional development sessions for teachers. He is Vice Chair of NALDIC and editor of its quarterly magazine.

Manny Vazquez is Head of Hounslow Language Service (for Secondary phase). He has worked in the field of EAL since 1979. His current responsibilities include EAL professional development and also teaching in a secondary school. He is a visiting lecturer for MA, PGCE and BEd courses and has been a speaker at international TESOL conferences. He has contributed to a range of professional journals, books and publications on the themes of language/content integration, and EAL assessment. He has also contributed towards DCSF materials on EAL for the National Strategy and on EAL assessment for QCA.

Alan Williams is a lecturer in the Faculty of Education at La Trobe University, Bundoora (Melbourne) Australia. He works in the area of TESOL methodology and curriculum. His research interests include content-based language teaching, the way culture is dealt with in TESOL, and approaches to teaching low literacy ESL/EAL learners. He has worked with teachers in schools and adult education programs. He has also worked as a classroom ESL teacher with a variety of learner groups, including low literacy ESL learners.

Foreword

While migration has been a constant in human development, the trans-border flow of peoples and languages witnessed since the late twentieth century has been remarkable in both scale and scope. Descriptors such as 'superdiversity' and the 'diversification of diversity' give an indication of the challenges faced by service providers in receiving countries across North America, much of Europe, Australia and New Zealand. Educators have found themselves at the forefront of efforts to meet needs.

Throughout this period, policy-makers have repeatedly failed to predict the resources and the strategies required to deal with new demands, responding in piecemeal fashion with bolt-on 'solutions'. One of the many unfortunate consequences of this pattern is the tendency to pathologize language learners; another is the failure to capitalize upon their strengths.

Meaningful ways forward have invariably come from reflective practitioners who have challenged received wisdom. On a national level, professional organizations have made it possible for individuals to exchange ideas and experiences. With the passage of time, we have come to realize that national issues are also international concerns and that it may be possible to adapt ideas developed in one location to other settings. This book represents the outcome of such national and international collaboration.

The different contributions embody many important principles. Firmly based on the realities of the classroom and written by practitioner-researchers, they look critically at top-down processes while reporting and reflecting on bottom-up processes. The aim is always to empower practitioners. Teacher autonomy and critical engagement with policies and the ideologies that underlie them form a recurrent theme. As such this book speaks powerfully to all who aspire to create learning opportunities for students in multilingual classrooms.

Viv Edwards
Professor of Language in Education
Director, National Centre for Language and Literacy
University of Reading

Preface

Marlena, a nine-year-old girl whose first language is Polish, is learning English as an additional language in an English school. When asked about this she describes the situation as she sees it:

> I think there are some children that can't speak English, some that quite can and some that perfectly can speak English. The slowest English learn is writing and the quickest is speak with your friends. (Marlena, Year 4, England)

Marlena, in her current context, is a linguistic minority student. In classrooms across the world, there are many Marlenas, learning English at the same time as tackling the particular curriculum skills and knowledge required in their classrooms, schools, states and national settings. Depending on location, they may be known as English Language Learners (ELLs), English as an Additional Language pupils, bilingual students or English as a Second Language Learners. For these young people, encounters with new and different languages are a 'given', a natural consequence of growing global mobility. For all its naturalness, maintaining linguistic diversity in English-dominant societies requires conscious effort, and professional experience everywhere has shown that teaching and learning English as an additional language is not just a common-sense enterprise. Like Marlena, the practitioners, teacher-educators and researchers who have contributed to this book recognize that there are challenges, and that these are, at once, local, national and supra-national. At the same time, the contributors know that their linguistically rich and diverse classrooms across Australia, Canada, England, the United States, and many other English-speaking places, peopled with 'vibrant and multi-faceted' students like Marlena, offer a host of opportunities. Wherever we are, the accounts in this book encourage us to create new and equitable learning opportunities for all of our students by exploring appropriate theory and research and by making local adaptations where necessary. This volume makes an important and timely contribution to the development and promotion of informed professional practice.

Nicola Davies
Chair of NALDIC

Introduction

Angela Creese and
Constant Leung

This book is intended for teachers working with linguistic minority pupils. Its chapters provide accounts of learning and teaching practices in classroom contexts in Australia, England and the United States. Our intention has been to present the work of practitioners, teacher-educators and researchers engaging in the daily practices of working with individuals, groups and whole classes through different approaches that are aimed at supporting students in linguistically rich and diverse classrooms. Each chapter describes an approach that is responsive to and positive about linguistic diversity and sets out guiding principles, examples, questions and further reading. The book aims to present to teachers an easy-to-use and accessible set of readings that provide ideas for adaptation to local contexts and circumstances. Each chapter works within a specific social and institutional context and invites readers to consider their own classrooms in relations to the pedagogic issues and approaches outlined. This book is relevant to all teachers who would like to increase their knowledge and skills and expand and evolve their responsibilities in relation to English language learners (ELL). Teachers are responsible for both the subject and linguistic/communicative needs of their students. As Pica suggests, 'World wide, teachers are confronted with the responsibility to teach classes of students who must acquire knowledge and skills in science, technology, business, and telecommunication, and do so through a language of which they know very little, or nothing at all.' (2008: 76). This book provides a guided discussion for teachers working with linguistic minority pupils.

The book cuts across national boundaries and illustrates what teachers share in their different national settings in working with linguistic minority students. It is through a focus on local classrooms that the possibilities of different approaches and educational principles can be considered. We believe that keeping things local helps mediate against what Denos et al. (2009) have described as imposed 'slots and categories' which damage the 'vibrant and multifaceted' young people with whom teachers work (2009: 37). Similarly, a focus on situated classroom practice allows teachers to consider themselves as agentive in bringing about change. Another study that illustrates the difference individual teachers can make in their linguistically diverse classrooms comes from Skilton-Sylvester (2003). She shows how different pedagogic approaches respond to the needs of children and adults studying English in US classrooms creating different learning opportunities. She argues that despite a prevailing language-as-a problem (Ruiz, 1984) orientation in US schools, teachers are able to create equitable educational practices for linguistically diverse students locally in their own classrooms. In the Skilton-Sylvester study teachers achieved this by adopting a positive and proactive stance towards the use of the Khmer language and culture in their classrooms. We hope the chapters in this book will also provide teachers with a sense of possibility and agency in creating learning opportunities for their students.

Another aspect shared across the chapters is an overarching competitive education system which underscores strong academic performance and emphasizes assessment in the subject matter, success in which allows students future educational opportunities. Language learning thus happens in an environment that is focused on subject curriculum. Stoller (2008: 65) argues that 'The integration of content and language-learning objectives presents challenges for policy makers, program planners, curriculum designers, teachers, materials writers, teacher educators, teacher supervisors, test writers, and learners.' These challenges run across all the national contexts described in this book. These include how best to align subject curriculum matter with language structures and functions and how best to sequence and select these language items from within a rich subject curriculum. The chapters share the common focus of education in compulsory school classrooms where young people have the dual aim of language learning and subject curriculum content learning.

As well as sharing understandings across national boundaries, there are also features that are unique to each. Terminology differs and chapter authors use various terms for describing learners, teachers and practices. These include English language learners (ELL), English as an additional language (EAL) pupil, bilingual students and English as a second language (ESL) learners, 'low literacy' learners, support teachers, EAL/ESL teachers, reading teachers. We have avoided trying to standardize these terms across the different chapters as we recognize that their development is context dependent, reflecting political debates about social practices in each national context. They reflect ideologies debated and contested in different nations. Moreover, different policy trajectories have created a whole range of policy acronyms particular to national contexts and we have made the decision to let these stand in each chapter with the author introducing and explaining specific terms where necessary.

The chapters presented in this book are about practice informed and guided by literature. They are accounts illustrating different pedagogic approaches grounded in specific classroom contexts. In each chapter local circumstances are described while simultaneously illustrating a particular orientation and approach to working with students learning English as an additional language (EAL) or second language (ESL) or bilingual students maintaining and enriching their community languages. These approaches include communicative approaches, bilingual approaches, content-based instructional approaches, sociocultural approaches and collaborative approaches. Each chapter provides a descriptive account of classroom life and invites the reader to extend this to their own classrooms in plausible and meaningful ways. We do not revisit earlier debates on 'approach', 'method' and 'technique'. Rather we orientate to recent work by Kumaravadivelu (2003) and arguments for postmethod pedagogy (see below). We will see in the chapters that follow authors taking up positions around the boundaries of the approaches they outline, with some viewing this as useful while others seeing the dangers.

Situated approaches to pedagogy: the postmethod condition

Our understanding of 'approach' views teachers as critical and reflective practitioners who adopt situated responses to their classroom contexts rather than taking up 'method packages'. In fact, current thinking describes the 'futility of searching for a method' (Kumaravadivelu, 2003: 23). Kumaravadivelu describes the term 'method' as limiting because it sets up hierarchies through which 'experts' in the field tell 'practitioners' what they should be doing. Rather, he suggests we should be seeking local and agentive responses to our classroom contexts based on guiding principles that build on our local and global social knowledge. He points out, 'The term *methods*, as currently used in the literature on second and foreign language (L2) teaching, does not refer to what teachers actually do in the classroom; rather it refers to established methods, conceptualized and constructed by experts in the field' (2003: 24). He describes several limitations of the concept of 'method' itself (2003: summarized from 28–30):

Over-idealization of the concept and context: Because methods are based on idealized concepts and geared towards idealized contexts they can never capture or visualize all the teaching needs, wants, and situations in advance. This means that teachers will not find situation-specific solutions in any one method. In other words, teachers need to be eclectic and adaptive in responding to their own students and their classroom needs.

Overly crude categories and boundaries: Kumaravadivelu explains how methods get caught up in what he describes as a 'whirlwind of fashion' (2003: 28). When this happens practitioners can end up adopting entrenched positions around the different approaches which do not necessarily help them to respond to their own local teaching and learning needs. Loyalty to one particular method can result in inflexible approaches as teachers align themselves to one rather than another method.

Failure to recognize 'eclectism' and pragmatism: This last limitation of 'method' presents the dangers of not thinking widely and broadly in terms of local needs. Because classroom teachers find it almost impossible to use any of the established methods as designed and delivered to them, they need to adapt. Kumaravadivelu argues they should adopt an eclectic approach that draws on whatever practical and intellectual resources teachers have available to them. However, Kumaravadivelu points out that the 'eclectic method' is rarely recognized or described in ELT Methods books.

This kind of argumentation leads Kumaravadivelu away from 'methods' towards what he calls the 'postmethod condition' (2003: 32–3). The postmethod condition signifies three interrelated attributes. First, it signifies a search for an alternative to method rather than an alternative method. While alternative methods are primarily products of top-down processes, alternatives to method are mainly products of bottom-up processes. According to Kumaravadivelu, the postmethod condition empowers practitioners to construct 'personal theories of practice' (2003: 33). Second, the postmethod condition signifies teacher autonomy which he describes as the ability of teachers to know how to develop a critical approach in order to self-observe, self-analyse, and self-evaluate their own teaching practice. The benefits of teacher autonomy are that teachers shape their own desired change and provide better opportunities for their students. The third attribute of the postmethod condition is principled pragmatism. Kumaravadivelu describes this as practice that sees the teacher responding to the immediacy of the local teaching context. We might think of this as teachers acknowledging their own values, beliefs and theories that come to shape their own pedagogic practices.

As described above, Kumaravadivelu describes the postmethod condition as a theory of practice in which macrostrategies should be used as principles to guide teachers working with students learning a second or additional language. These macrostrategies are 'derived from historical, theoretical, empirical and experiential insights related to L2 learning and teaching' (2003: 38). Kumaravadivelu describes these macrostrategies as providing a general plan or a broad set of guidelines for generating one's own situation-specific micros-trategies or classroom techniques. Thus macrostrategies are always supple-mented with microstaegies, which are responses to local circumstances. Kumaravadivelu lists ten macrostrategies. They are produced in full below (2003: 39–40). In the chapters that follow we see many of these macrostrate-gies illustrated in action as well as microstrategies particular to specific class-rooms. In listing the macrostrategies below we also provide an example from one of the chapters in this book to illustrate the key point behind each macros-trategy. Each chapter contains a plethora of further examples.

Maximize learning opportunities: This macrostrategy envisages teaching as a process of creating and utilizing learning opportunities, a process in which teachers strike a balance between their role as managers of teaching acts and their role as mediators of learning acts. In Chapter 6 we see how two different teachers in two different classrooms use the pedagogical structure of 'Reciprocal Teaching' to mediate the joint learning aims of language and subject content. The teachers balance the curriculum so that both a language and content focus is possible while addressing the management of all the different needs of the students in their classes.

Minimize perceptual mismatches: This macrostrategy emphasizes the recognition of potential perceptual mismatches between intentions and interpretations of the learner; the teacher; and the teacher-educator. In Chapter 2 we learn how inclusive pedagogies, unless properly resourced with appropriate teacher expertise and knowledge may fail the very students they set out to support. Mismatches between the rhetoric of inclusion and the sometimes excluding practices of classroom life illustrate how linguistically diverse students learning English as an additional language might suffer.

Facilitate negotiated interaction: This macrostrategy refers to meaningful learner-learner, learner-teacher classroom interaction in which learners are entitled and encouraged to initiate topics and talk, not just react and respond; Chapters 2 and 5 describe how teachers in partnerships bring different interactional possibilities and opportunities for teaching and learning in the way they interact with students. Chapter 7 shows how teachers with different specialisms, for example EAL and subject teachers use language differently in working with linguistically diverse students and discusses the possibilities of different interactional styles.

Promote learner autonomy: This macrostrategy involves helping learners learn how to learn, equipping them with the means necessary to self-direct and self-monitor their own learning; Chapter 7 provides positive examples of how teachers can bring together learning from the home with learning at school so that young people come to view their own experiences as valuable in shaping their own development.

Foster language awareness: This macrostrategy refers to any attempt to draw learners' attention to the formal and functional properties of their L2 in order to increase the degree of explicitness required to promote L2 learning. Chapter 3 describes approaches that show one particular student becoming aware of the language and subject knowledge necessary in order to progress in her examinations. This chapter shows how a teacher can make explicit the language required for examination success.

Activate intuitive heuristics and *contextualize linguistic input:* These two macro-strategies are both concerned with the importance of providing rich textual data so that learners can infer and internalize underlying rules governing grammatical usage and communicative use. They highlight how language usage and use are shaped by linguistic, extralinguistic, situational and extrasituational contexts. These two macrostrategies are exemplified in Chapter 6 which shows how teachers make connections between language content and linguistic knowledge, illustrating along the way how teachers can use texts for meeting the dual learning aims of language usage and communicative use. A focus on language allows for a focus on both grammar and its role in meaning-making.

Integrate language skills: This microstrategy refers to the need to holistically integrate language skills traditionally separated and sequenced as listening, speaking, reading and writing. Chapter 5 shows the importance of holistic integration but also the dangers of subsuming the individual language skills within the subject curriculum paradigm which in many classrooms does not allow an opportunity for a language focus. When this happens, the traditional skills are holistically integrated into the subject focus but are often lost entirely as the teacher engages in subject transmission.

Ensure social relevance: This macrostrategy refers to the need for teachers to be sensitive to the societal, political, economic and educational environment in which L2 learning and teaching take place. Chapter 7 illustrates how classroom practices must draw in the outside worlds of their students and bring these into the classroom to create more equal learning environments which validate and represent students' cultural and social experiences. Chapter 4 illustrates how the wider social and political context in Australia has created the need for a nuanced response to a particular group of students described as 'low literacy'. Chapter 4 shows how the educational response needs to take into account the experiences of these learners whose histories are those of disrupted education.

Raise cultural consciousness: This macrostrategy emphasizes the need to treat learners as cultural informants so that they are encouraged to engage in a process of classroom participation that puts a premium on their power/knowledge. Chapter 8 articulates the importance of affirming identities, promoting bilingualism and fostering integration as central to every level of decision-making in the classroom. The chapter emphasizes the importance of responding to the linguistic and cultural diversity of bilingual students in our classrooms as a positive resource.

Method dogma

Kumaravadivelu's framework of principles, macrostrategies and microstrategies are proposed to counter what some have called the dogma of methods (McKay, 2002). The application of methods 'carte blanche' leads to unthinking teachers (see Leung and Creese, Concluing Remarks). Shohamy (2006) has described how teachers can serve as soldiers of the system carrying out orders without questioning policy and the ideologies and agendas behind it. Van Deusen-Scholl (2008: xvii) suggests that teachers should view themselves as part of the bigger social and political picture and 'the multiple goals and purposes of language education within plurilingual/pluricultural environments'. McKay (2002) points to the importance of considering teacher beliefs and values and argues that this needs to be the starting point in considering what methods might work in any particular classroom. Quoting Prabhu (1990), McKay suggests that we start with what is *plausible* for the teacher. This is because teachers bring a subjective interpretation to their teaching context and make sense of the method through their own sense of plausibility. As McKay puts it (2002: 116):

> This sense of plausibility is influenced by teachers' own experience in the past as learners, by their experience of teaching, and by their exposure to one or more teaching methods. A method then, for Prabhu is 'a highly

developed and highly articulated sense of plausibility (1990: 175). Thus, 'the best method varies from one teacher to another, but only in the sense that it is best for each teacher to operate with his or her own sense of plausibility at any given time' (ibid: 175–6).

The literature we have reviewed here reinforces the importance of local interpretations of theory and research for producing responsive classrooms through informed practice. It places teachers at the centre of their classrooms in creating cultures of learning that are meaningful and plausible to them and therefore to their students. This view offers those of us working in linguistically diverse educational contexts proactive and local strategies for shaping our classrooms. It emphasizes the ability of practitioners to change and transform settings. It asks us to think local and consider how our own practices as teachers and researchers will figure in the lives of the students we work with. Kramsch and Sullivan describe this as 'global thinking, local teaching' (1996: 200).

All of the eight chapters that follow document a theory into practice approach and show it in action. Each chapter describes a different context but all share the aim of exemplification. They illustrate language educators drawing on applied linguistic research to illuminate and solve problems they encounter in their practice (Kramsch, 2008). They describe many of the challenges faced by teachers in educational contexts which typically view linguistically diverse classrooms as sites of social problems rather than sites of social resource (Ruiz, 1984). The chapters offer contextualized accounts of teachers' resistance to negative constructions of linguistic diversity and provide examples of response, personalization and differentiation. They show teachers addressing common and individual needs of their diverse students.

Chapter 1 comes from Constant Leung who outlines the principles and interpretations of communicative language teaching (CLT). He provides an overview of the theoretical influences on CLT and describes how this has been interpreted in practice particularly in English schools. In this chapter the functional perspective inherent in CLT, in which language is viewed as performing a set of different functions, is described. Leung considers CLT's relevance to subject content teaching and its conduciveness for EAL development. His chapter introduces four chapters that show learning and teaching contexts broadly influenced by the CLT paradigm. Although it has been seriously critiqued, CLT continues to have a tremendous influence on all language teaching fields of research, policy and practice (EAL, EFL, ESL, MFL[1] and community languages). Over 20 years ago, Swan expressed his concern about the communicative language teaching (CLT) canon.

Along with its many virtues, the Communicative Approach unfortunately has most of the typical vices of an intellectual revolution: it over-generalizes valid but limited insights until they become virtually meaningless; it makes exaggerated claims for the power and novelty of its doctrines; it misrepresents the currents of thought it has replaced; it is often characterized by serious intellectual confusions; it is choked with jargon. (Swan 1985: 2 cited in McKay, 2002: 111; also see Leung, 2005 for a further discussion.)

While CLT's limitations have become increasingly clear its relevance to those teaching languages is still hugely important. Van Deusen-Scholl describes new avenues in CLT approaches.

> New approaches have attempted to address these concerns while maintaining a communicative focus, emphasizing a highly interactive learning environment, and increasingly providing a more authentic context for learning. Several authors point out the limitations of the ways communicative language teaching has been applied as too utilitarian and suggest new perspectives which take into consideration the social and cultural context. (Van Deusen-Scholl, 2008: xiv)

The chapters that follow show how CLT influences are moulded and shaped by both local and wider social contexts. Frank Monaghan considers the mainstream classroom as a site for language learning. He provides a historical, social and political account of current policy and outlines how teachers and teaching, and learners and learning are conceptualized in policy. The chapter considers what teacher professional knowledge and skills are involved in working with students learning English as an additional language (EAL) and makes important points about teacher collaboration, pedagogy and knowledge. Manny Vazquez uses an extended anecdote to consider the relevance of research evidence. He places himself and his student Mona at the heart of the chapter in a process of discovery and reflection. Using research evidence produced by Lynne Cameron (2002) he exemplifies how he adapts and responds to his student's vocabulary learning needs from within the national assessment system. Alan Williams describes what English as a second language (ESL) teachers need to know when responding to a particular group of students who face significant challenges in Australian schools. Williams shows how 'low literacy' ESL learners need particular responses beyond those typically labelled ESL. Using theory that views literacy as social practice, he shows how teachers can respond to both the autonomous and ideological dimensions of literacy. Angela Creese investigates how certain pedagogies come to have more power and authority than others. She does this by analysing the interactions of different teachers working with different students. Candace Harper, Kimberly Cook and Carol James describe the integration of content and language in American classrooms. Using an instruction technique called reciprocal teaching they illustrate how two different classrooms balance content and language learning aims. The chapter shows how the two teachers activate and develop students' background knowledge, increase participation and make connections in discussions of text. The chapter considers factors that affect teachers' ability to respond to the dual demands of language and content foci. Margaret Hawkins describes a sociocultural approach to language teaching and learning. She shows the importance of considering language use as situated in the community. Hawkins illustrates the importance of schools valuing and validating all the languages and cultures of its community and goes on to illustrate how teachers might achieve this. She demonstrates this through introducing the reader to two fictional students who are being inducted into different school projects. Hawkins shows some of the challenges that might arise for these students and considers how teachers might respond. De Jong and Freeman Field describe bilingual approaches in education and show how educators can achieve quality schooling for bilingual learners through the use of three principles: affirming linguistic and cultural identities; promoting additive bilingualism; and fostering integration. Like the previous chapters, they illustrate these principles in practice through accounts of classroom life.

Note

1 English as an additional language, English as foreign language, English as a second language, modern foreign language.

References

Cameron, L. (2002) 'Measuring vocabulary size in English as an additional language', *Language Teaching Research*, 6 (2): 145–73.

Denos, C., Toohey, K., Neilson, K. and Waterston, B. (2009) *Collaborative Research in Multilingual Classrooms*. Clevedon: Multilingual Matters.

García, O. (2005) 'Positioning heritage languages in the United States', *The Modern Language Journal*, 89: 601–5.

Hornberger, N. H. (2001) 'Multilingual literacies, literacy practices, and the continua of biliteracy', in M. Martin-Jones and K. Jones (eds), *Multilingual Literacies: Reading and Writing in Different Worlds*. Amsterdam: John Benjamins pp. 353–67.

Hornberger, N. and Skilton-Sylvester, E. (2000) 'Revisiting the continua of biliteracy: International and critical perspective', *Language and Education*, 14: 96–122.

Kramsch, C. (2008) 'Applied linguistic theory and second/foreign language education', in N. Van Deusen-Scholl and N. H. Hornberger (eds), *Encyclopedia of Language and Education*, 2nd edn, Vol. 4: Second and Foreign Language Education. New York: Springer Science/Business Media LLC pp. 3–16.

Kramsch, C. and Sullivan, P. (1996) 'Appropriate pedagogy', *ELT Journal*, 50: 199–212.

Kumaravadivelu, B. (2003) *Beyond Methods: Macrostrategies for Language Teaching*. New Haven, CT and London: Yale University Press.

Leung, C. (2005) 'Convivial communication: recontextualizing communicative competence', *International Journal of Applied Linguistics*, 15 (2): 119–44.

McKay, S. Lee (2002) *Teaching English as an International Language*. Oxford: Oxford University Press.

Pica, T. (2008) 'Task-based instruction', in N. Van Deusen-Scholl and N. H. Hornberger (eds), *Encyclopedia of Language and Education*, 2nd edn, Vol. 4: Second and Foreign Language Education. New York: Springer Science/Business Media LLC pp. 71–82.

Prabhu, N. S. (1990) 'There is no best method – why?' *TESOL Quarterly*, 24 (2): 161–76.

Ruiz, R. (1984) 'Orientations in language planning', *NABE Journal*, 8 (2): 15–34.

Shohamy, E. (2006) *Language Policy: Hidden Agendas and New Approaches*. Abingdon and New York: Routledge.

Skilton-Sylvester, E. (2002) 'Should I stay or should I go? Investigating Cambodian women's participation and investment in adult ESL programs', *Adult Education Quarterly*, 53 (1): 9–26.

Stoller, F. L. (2008) 'Content-based instruction', in N. Van Deusen-Scholl and N. H. Hornberger (eds), *Encyclopedia of Language and Education*, 2nd edn, Vol. 4: Second and Foreign Language Education. New York: Springer Science/ Business Media LLC pp. 59–70.

Swan, M. (1985) 'A critical look at the communicative approach (2)', *ELT Journal*, 39 (1): 76–87.

Van Deusen-Scholl, N. (2008) 'Introduction to Volume 4: Second and Foreign Language Education', in N. Van Deusen-Scholl and N. H. Hornberger (eds), *Encyclopedia of Language and Education*, 2nd edn, Vol. 4: Second and Foreign Language Education. New York: Springer Science/Business Media LLC pp. xiii–xx.

1

Communicative Language Teaching and EAL: Principles and Interpretations

Constant Leung

Introduction

In the past 50 years many English-speaking countries such as Australia, Britain, Canada and the USA have seen large-scale movements of people across national and language borders. These societies now have linguistically diverse school populations. For instance, in England about 13.5 per cent of the primary (elementary) school population is regarded as learners and users of English as an Additional Language (National Statistics, 2007), and in California 25 per cent of the school population is classified as English Language Learners (similar to ESL/EAL) (EdSource, 2008). Different education systems have responded to this growing trend of linguistic diversity in different ways (see Leung, 2007; Leung and Creese, 2008 for a detailed discussion). There is a variety of approaches to English language teaching for EAL learners. In some systems intensive initial EAL tuition is provided for new arrivals, in other places the main response is to make the mainstream (meaning the ordinary) school curriculum as accessible to EAL learners as possible. The latter approach is premised on the proposition that if EAL learners can participate in ordinary subject teaching-learning activities, then English language learning will follow. In this and the next three chapters of the book we will focus on the ideas and principles associated with classroom communication and participation, with particular reference to additional/second language.

The teaching of English language, both as mother tongue and as an additional language, since the mid-1970s has been in numerous ways associated with the concept of Communicative Language Teaching.[1] The ideas underpinning this concept first emerged in the early 1970s and they represented a major shift from a view of language (and language teaching) that was primarily concerned with vocabulary and grammar. In this chapter I first present a brief account of the theoretical bases of the notion of language as communication in social

1

contexts. This is followed by a discussion on the influence of these ideas by looking at some examples of language teaching approaches which prioritize the social nature of 'communication' (rather than other formal aspects of language such as grammar). In the final section I suggest that the concept of Communicative Language Teaching has turned out to be a broad church, so to speak. On the one hand, the very powerful core ideas at the heart of this concept can be adopted in a variety of teaching contexts. On the other hand, our collective professional experience has shown that the broad principles of Communicative Language Teaching need to be adapted and extended in local contexts, if teachers are to meet the language learning needs of their students. Chapters 2, 3, 4 and 5 will provide four situated accounts of how Communicative Language Teaching has worked in practice and the pedagogic issues that this approach has engendered.

Language functions in communication

It has been widely acknowledged that the work of Halliday and his colleagues in the early 1970s represents a significant move to a socially oriented conceptualization of language and language teaching (e.g. Howatt and Widdowson, 2004: Chapter 20). Central to this conceptualization is the idea of 'language function'. Function is understood in terms of the relationship between meaning and linguistic form. What we, as language users, mean to express in speech and writing is realized by the specific linguistic resources (e.g. words and clauses/sentences) we select to represent our meaning. By the same token, what we say or write *is* what we mean. Thus, meaning and linguistic form are mutually constituting. This functional relationship 'reflects the fact that language has evolved in the service of particular human needs ... what is really significant is that this functional principle is carried over and built into the grammar, so that the internal organization of the grammatical system is also functional in character' (Halliday, 1975: 16). A practical example of what this means is to consider a statement such as 'The Prime Minister said an extra £50 million pounds will be spent on school improvement.' The same propositional meaning can be expressed in many other ways, for example: 'The Government promises an additional ...', 'An extra £50 million pounds will be put into school improvement', and so on. Each of these statements conveys the same 'basic' information, but the variations in vocabulary and grammar signal different emphases in meaning, which are an important aspect of message-conveying through language expressions. The speaker/writer of these statements would have different communicative purposes in mind. (This point will be further elaborated in a later section.) This view represents a major departure from the more conventional view of language that regards language as some sort of autonomous linguistic system that (a) has universal norms of correctness and (b) has an existence independently of human language users and their needs. In passing perhaps we should note that this autonomous view has been very powerful. The persistent calls to teaching students to learn to use grammar rules of the so-called Standard English correctly, irrespective of context and purpose of communication, is a good example of this enduring view.

A fundamental assumption in this Hallidayan functional view of language is that what people choose to mean and say is open-ended. There are infinite options in meaning-making and these options are categorized in terms of three functional components (often referred to as metafunctions in the Hallidayan literature): ideational, interpersonal and textual. The ideational component refers to the aspect of language use where 'the speaker expresses his experience of the phenomena of the external world, and of the internal world of his own consciousness' (1975: 17). When people describe events and feelings, the substantive content of what they are describing can be regarded as ideational meaning. The interpersonal component is concerned with the 'function of language as a means whereby the speaker participates in ... [a] speech situation' (1975: 17). This is the aspect of language use in which social relationships are expressed; speakers can adopt or perform a role in relation to other participants (as friends or as teachers and so on). The textual component represents an 'enabling function ... the function that language has of creating text' (1975: 17). Put differently, it is concerned with the use and organization of linguistic resources, in the broadest sense, to create a spoken or written message (however long or short, complex or simple) to make meaning in context. It should be stressed that these functional components are analytical categories. In real-life language communication, they occur simultaneously in speech or writing in specific social contexts. (For a fuller discussion of systemic functional grammar see for instance Halliday and Matthiessen, 2000; Halliday, 2004.)

Communicative competence

Another major influence on the development of Communicative Language Teaching was the work of Hymes (1972, 1977) on communicative competence within the tradition of ethnography of communication. His 1972 paper 'On Communicative Competence' (first presented in 1966 as a conference paper) explicitly addressed language education issues. It was in part a critique of Chomsky's (1965) highly abstracted notion of grammatical competence which can be associated with an autonomous view of language discussed in the last section. It was intended as a clarion call to language educators to pay attention to the fact that what counts as competence in language communication can vary within a speech community, let alone cross different speech communities; there is '*differential competence* within a *heterogeneous speech community*, both undoubtedly shaped by acculturation' (Hymes, 1972: 274, original italics).

For Hymes (1972: 277), children learning to communicate through language have to develop a language knowledge (vocabulary and grammar) as well as rules of appropriate use. They need to learn when and how to speak, what to talk about with whom, and so on. In other words, there are social rules of use 'without which the rules of grammar would be useless' (Hymes, 1972: 278). This inclusion of the 'social' makes it necessary to raise questions of context of communication and aspects of sociocultural practice when teaching language. To determine what counts as communicative competence, four real-life language questions must be asked:

> Whether (and to what degree) something is formally **possible**;
> Whether (and to what degree) something is **feasible** in virtue of the means of implementation available;
> Whether (and to what degree) something is **appropriate** (adequate, happy, successful) in relation to a context in which it is used and evaluated;
> Whether (and to what degree) something is in fact done, actually **performed**, and what its doing entails. (Hymes, 1972: 281, original emphasis)

This way of conceptualizing the notion of communicative competence offered language educators a dynamic and socially grounded perspective on language and language use. Canale and Swain produced a series of seminal papers in the early 1980s that rendered the Hymesian ideas in more language education terms with particular reference to additional language (Canale, 1983, 1984, Canale and Swain, 1980a, 1980b). In their account communicative competence comprises four areas or 'component' competences of knowledge and skills:

(1) *Grammatical competence*: this is concerned with the use of 'knowledge of lexical items and of rules of morphology, syntax, sentence-grammar semantics, and phonology' (Canale and Swain, 1980a: 29). This type of knowledge and skill allows the language learner to make use of language resources to understand and create propositional meaning.

(2) *Sociolinguistic competence*: this is concerned with rules of use, including the probability of 'whether (and to what degree) something is in fact done' (Hymes, 1972: 281), that is, whether something is 'sayable' in a given context, from the point of view of participant members of a particular community.

> [It] addresses the extent to which utterances are produced and understood appropriately in different sociolinguistic contexts depending on contextual factors such as status of participants, purposes of the interaction, and norms or conventions of interaction ... Appropriateness of utterances refers to ... appropriateness of meaning and appropriateness of meaning concerns the extent to which particular communicative functions (e.g. commanding, complaining and inviting), attitudes (including politeness and formality) and ideas are judged to be proper in a given situation. (Canale, 1983: 7)

(3) *Discourse competence*: this is concerned with organizational features of spoken and written texts (of any kind). There are two elements in this competence: cohesion (Halliday and Hasan, 1976), and coherence (Widdowson, 1978). Different types of texts, such as oral and written narratives, diaries, and scientific reports, tend to combine grammatical forms with selected meanings in particular ways.

> Unity of a text is achieved through cohesion in form and coherence in meaning. Cohesion deals with how utterances are linked structurally and facilitates interpretation of a text. For example, the use of cohesion devices such as pronoun, synonyms ... Coherence refers to the relationship among the different meanings in a text, where these meanings may be literal meanings, communicative functions and attitudes. (Canale, 1983: 9)

(4) *Strategic competence*: this is concerned with additional language learners' capacity to communicate by using verbal and non-verbal strategies (a) to compensate for breakdowns in communication due to a lack of language knowledge or momentary memory limitation (or other psycho-cognitive issues); and (b) to enhance communication (e.g. use of slow speech for rhetorical effect). (Canale, 1983: 11)

This formulation of communicative competence expanded the conceptual base of additional/second/foreign language curriculum and pedagogy that existed up until the late 1970s in countries such as the USA and the UK. It is no exaggeration to say that the Canale and Swain analytic account of communicative competence very quickly became the theoretical and curriculum basis of the emerging Communicative Language Teaching approach in the early 1980s, particularly in the worldwide enterprise of teaching English to speakers of other languages. Over the years the label Communicative Language Teaching has been interpreted and reworked in various ways. But as a conceptualization of language, as a general curriculum principle, and as a teaching approach, it has remained a central concern in the work of language teachers, curriculum planners, textbook writers, and, last but not least, researchers in language education (for instance Bachman, 1990; Brown, 2000; Brumfit, 1984; Burns, 2005; Council of Europe, 2001; QCA, 2007;[2] Widdowson, 1975, 1978, among many others).

Theory into practice

The central ideas in the two bodies of work discussed above have inspired and influenced numerous curriculum designs and material development projects. A brief description of some examples is provided here.[3] As part of the preparation for the introduction of the National Curriculum in England and Wales, the curriculum authorities commissioned the Language in the National Curriculum project (LINC, 1989–92) in the late 1980s.[4] (For further details, see Carter, 1997; Carter and McRae, 1996; Carter and Nash, 1990.) The brief for this initiative was to produce teacher education material that would support the teaching of English in school within the statutory National Curriculum in England and Wales in the early 1990s. LINC (1989–92: 3) took the view that

> pupils' language development can be more effectively supported if teachers know more about the systematic organisation and function of language ... The purpose of the LINC material is to give teachers greater analytic knowledge about language across all areas ... forms and structures of language; relationships between speakers and listener between writer and reader ...

This material, covering both spoken and written language, draws on the Hallidayan functional perspective. For instance, in one teaching activity on the theme of 'variations in written language' for senior secondary students, teachers are asked to develop a text-type game involving the following steps:

Material preparation: The teacher cuts up three groups of labels of writing purposes (e.g. Complain, Inform, Describe), audience (e.g. Teacher, Police Officer, Unknown Person), and text types (e.g. Report, Recipe, Personal Letter) and puts them in three piles.

In-class activities: The teacher shuffles the three piles of cards and puts them face down on a table, then turns up the top card in each pile one by one. The random ordering of the cards may now turn up in unpredictable and unexpected combinations, such as Complain-Recipe-Unknown Person (whereas Complain-Report-Police Officer may be more customarily expected). The unexpected combinations of purpose audience and text types can be used as discussion points. The teacher can also use the various combinations of text and audience to lead a discussion on questions such as: Should spoken or written language be used and under what circumstances? What written or spoken language conventions should be adopted? This teaching activity is clearly informed by a functional view of language use that relates language form to purpose and context in a systematic way. (For further details, see LINC, 1989–92: 156.)

This functional perspective was also adopted in the development of the genre theory approach to teaching school literacy that emerged in approximately the same period (the mid-to-late 1980s) in Australia.[5] 'Genre' has been understood in several senses in the related fields of language studies, linguistics and literature. The sense in which the term 'genre' is used in this particular body of work is related to the functional view of language discussed earlier. The functional relationship between meaning and language expressions at the clause or sentence level is now extended to the whole text level. On this view, there are socially and culturally powerful texts that deploy language resources (vocabulary, grammar and rhetorical organization) in recognized ways. These context- and purpose-oriented ways of using language, particularly written language, are held to be sedimented into recognizable patterns. The term 'literacy' used in this particular body of work does not exclude talk, but the main focus is primarily on the use of written language for social and institutional purposes. Cope and Kalantzis (1993: 67), for instance, argue that:

> writing and speaking have distinctively different linguistic structures; and different ways of using language have different social effect. Literacy, and the types of transformation of oral language that come with literacy, open linguistic doors into certain realms of social action and social power. It follows that literacy teaching, if it is to provide students with equitable social access, needs to link the different social purposes of language in different contexts to predict patterns of discourse.

These predictable patterns of discourse are found in socially powerful texts at different levels of society and in different social institutions. These texts tend to conform to '[g]enres [which] are conventional structures which have evolved as pragmatic schemes for making certain types of meaning and to achieve distinctive social goals, in specific settings, by particular linguistic means' (1993: 67). For the purposes of language teaching this perspective would call for close attention to how school texts are constructed. Veel (1997), for example, suggests that school science texts tend to follow a knowledge trajectory that starts with the genres related to doing science (for instance, procedures for doing experiments), which is followed by explaining science (causal explanations), organizing scientific information (descriptive and taxonomic reports), and challenging science (exposition of argument for or against an issue). A similar shift from the concrete to the abstract in school history – from history as story to history as argument – has also been identified by Coffin (1997). Each of these science or history activities is associated with a particular genre(s). By examining how language resources are deployed in the formation of a text in particular subject areas, teachers can help make writing (and reading) more transparent.

Schleppegrell et al. (2004) offer an example of how this functional perspective can work to help unpack subject content meaning. Additional/second language students often find the particular ways in which English language wording is used in different academic subjects difficult. This domain or subject specific use of language is often referred to as 'register'. Schleppegrell and her colleagues look at ways of helping teachers make subject texts accessible for English as an additional language students. In this case the subject is history in middle school in the United States. Using a Hallidayan approach that regards meaning and language expressions in a mutually constituting relationship (see earlier discussion on 'function'), they examine how lexical and grammatical resources are used in school history texts and how explicit discussion on the language of history texts can help students to unpack complex meanings. For instance, one needs to be able to identify events and happenings in history texts (ideational meaning); happenings and events tend to be encoded in action verbs of processes. But history texts comprise more than 'factual' statements on events; they also contain statements of judgement and persuasion (interpersonal meaning). Therefore it is argued that helping students to understand that there are different types of verbs and that they serve different functions is a useful pedagogic move.

> The verbs used in writing about history can be classified as action verbs such as *fight, defend, build, vote* and so forth; saying and thinking-feeling verbs such as *said, expressed, supposed, like, resent,* and so forth; and relating verbs such as *is, have, is called,* and so forth. This categorization helps students understand when authors are writing about events (action verbs), when they are giving opinions or telling what others have said (thinking-feeling and saying verbs), and when they are giving background information (relating verbs). (Schleppegrell et al., 2004: 77)

Furthermore, actors and agents (referred to as participants in functional grammatical analysis) are important in history, but they can be difficult to identify sometimes. At a sentence level, for instance, in a statement such as 'Liverpool's slave trade accounted for 15 per cent of Britain's entire overseas trade by the end of the eighteenth century', it is not clear who the actors were. In fact it is difficult to see what actions and events might be involved in 'overseas trade'. The use of abstract nouns or noun phrases as participants may be conceptually apt as a means of conveying complex historical events and processes, but the language text expressing this kind of meaning can be difficult to decipher. Functional grammatical analysis, with its focus on the relationship between content meaning and language expression, can help to draw attention to abstract and complex expressions that need unpacking.

Communication and language learning

One key pedagogic point to emerge from the ideas discussed in the previous sections is that language learning is more than just learning the English language as vocabulary and grammar as discrete bodies of knowledge. Learning to understand and use language in ways that are appropriate in context (in accordance with the language practices of a particular community in question) is equally important. Given that language teachers and learners are not researchers and that they cannot know every possible communicative situation which their students may encounter, an interesting question here is what constitutes Communicative Language Teaching in the classroom. For example, Brown (2001: 43) offers a set of characteristics that includes the following:[6]

- attending to 'the components (grammatical, discourse, functional, socio-linguistic, and strategic) of communicative competence';
- using activities and tasks that would 'engage learners in the pragmatic, authentic, functional use of language for meaningful purposes';
- '[s]tudents are therefore encouraged to construct meaning through genuine linguistic interaction with others'.

These characteristics suggest that, instead of finding out what people actually do when they use language to communicate with one another in specific contexts, Communicative Language Teaching has turned its focus to creating language-using activities in the classroom to facilitate practice in communication (for a fuller discussion, see Leung, 2005).

The term Communicative Language Teaching is not often explicitly invoked in EAL programmes and teacher education materials.[7] This is, however, not to say that the general principles underpinning Communicative Language Teaching have not made any impact. In fact, many of the early well-known EAL teaching approaches, such as Cognitive Academic Language Learning (CALLA) (Chamot and O'Malley, 1987) and the Topics Approach (Evans, 1986; Evans and Cleland, no date), place a good deal of emphasis on the idea that students should (a) be directly engaged in doing curriculum tasks and communicating with others (through spoken or written modes) at the same time; and (b) be given the opportunity to learn and rehearse the necessary and relevant language related to the tasks.

English as an Additional Language in the mainstream curriculum

The mainstream (ordinary) curriculum is the place where a good deal of EAL teaching and learning is meant to take place, particularly for those students who are beyond the early stages of learning English (see Leung, 2007, Leung and Creese, 2008 for a detailed discussion) in many English-speaking education systems. Given that the mainstream curriculum is primarily concerned with other areas of subject learning (including the subject of English which, among others things, has literature as content), how far can we describe it as an EAL teaching-learning environment? Again, although the term Communicative Language Learning has not been routinely and explicitly used in mainstream curriculum and teacher guidance documents, nevertheless the notion of communication, as characterized in the last section, lies at the heart of the thinking that the mainstream classroom can be made into a productive environment for EAL development. For instance, an early National Curriculum Council (England) (NCC, 1991: 2) directive to teachers advised them that they should adopt a range of teaching techniques that would allow EAL students to participate and to communicate in classroom learning activities which included these:

- Matrices, true/false exercises, data presentations and other display work can help to ensure that achievement is not entirely dependent on proficiency in English.
- Exercises with some repetitive element ... provide a pattern that supports language development.
- The use of familiar objects provides first-hand experience and does not require sophisticated language skills.

The pedagogic value of participation embedded in this 1991 directive has been repeated in many other teacher guidance and advice documents. For instance, in a recent guidance document school inspectors are told that

> All EAL learners have a right to access the National Curriculum and the Early Years Foundation Stage. This is best achieved within a whole school context. Pupils learn more quickly when socialising and interacting with their peers who speak English fluently and can provide good language and learning role models. (OFSTED, 2008: 17)

In the National Curriculum programme of study for secondary school students in England one of the key concepts for the subject English (QCA, 2007: 69) is 'competence' which is defined as follows:

(a) Being clear, coherent and accurate in spoken and written communication.
(b) Reading and understanding a range of texts, and responding appropriately.
(c) Demonstrating a secure understanding of the conventions of written language, including grammar, spelling and punctuation.
(d) Being adaptable in a widening range of familiar and unfamiliar contexts within the classroom and beyond.
(e) Making informed choices about effective ways to communicate formally and informally.

Terms and phrases such as 'communication', 'responding appropriately', 'making informed choices about effective ways to communicate formally and informally' and so on quite clearly echo the concerns of Halliday, Hymes, Canale and Swain, and others discussed earlier. So, on the face of it, the mainstream classroom is, arguably, potentially a very conducive environment for EAL development. It is communicatively active, full of interactions and activities, and the use of language is (meant to be) purposeful. The next four chapters will draw on professional experience to examine the affordances and pitfalls of the Communicative Language Teaching approach from an EAL perspective. Frank Monaghan and Manny Vazquez explore some of the language learning issues that have arisen in the English schooling education context. Alan Williams examines some of the issues faced by teachers and curriculum planners when working with particular groups of school students with 'low literacy' backgrounds in ESL programmes in an Australian context. Angela Creese, working in an English context, looks at a range of pedagogic issues related to some underexplored, indeed hidden, tensions in terms of curriculum focus and priorities when subject teachers and EAL teachers are meant to be collaborating. In different ways these authors are concerned with questions such as:

• How far does 'everyday' classroom communication meet students' additional language learning needs?
• Does 'communication' in general provide the requisite language learning opportunities for subject specific academic language?

- Does classroom communication provide the necessary cultural/transcultural learning that is required for different groups of EAL learners with different backgrounds?

Points for reflection

1 Hymes's notion of communicative competence suggests that proficient use of language should be grammatically accurate and socially appropriate. How might this notion be put into practice in EAL teaching, particularly in the context of a subject classroom (for example, science)?
2 In Halliday's view any instance of language use serves three meta-functions (ideational, interpersonal and textual). How might these be taken into account when teaching EAL?

Suggestions for further reading

Burns, A. (ed.) (2005) *Teaching English from a Global Perspective*. Alexandria, VA: Teachers of English to Speakers of Other Languages, Inc.
Genesee, F. (ed.) (1994) *Educating Second Language Children*. Cambridge: Cambridge University Press.
McKay, S. L. and Bokhorst-Heng, W. D. (2008) *International English in its Sociolinguistic Contexts: Towards a Socially Sensitive EIL Pedagogy*. Abingdon: Routledge.

Notes

1 It is understood that the school subject English in English-speaking countries and English-medium international schools normally comprises the study of English language (often referred to as Use of English) and literature in English. This discussion focuses on the aspects of English that are linked to language use, not literature.
2 Some traces of this concept can be found in the 2008 version of the English National Curriculum (QCA, 2007: 47), a curriculum designed with the mainstream school population in mind.
3 For reasons of space and scope, only examples of use of English in school curriculum-related projects will be discussed here. There are countless examples of Communicative Language Teaching in fields such as English as a Foreign Language.
4 The work produced by the LINC project was not officially published because policy-makers at the time did not consider the material fit for purpose. 'When this in-service programme was reviewed at the end of 1991, it was decided by the government of the day that it was insufficiently formal and decontextualised

in character and failed to pay sufficient attention to the rules of standard English. As a result and against a background of considerable public dispute, the government decided against publication but allowed the materials to be distributed in *samizdat* form for purposes of continuing training' (Carter, www. phon.ucl.ac.uk/home/dick/ec/linc.htm, accessed 15 January 2009).

5 There are other genre approaches that have different theoretical foundations, see Bazerman (2004), Hyon (1996), Swales (1990), among others.

6 Brown's account is oriented towards teachers of English as a Foreign Language. The characterizations made are, however, equally valid for the purpose of this discussion.

7 In contrast, in the field of English as a Foreign Language, the term Communicative Language Teaching is widely used to promote course books, language classes and language tests.

References

Bachman, L. (1990) *Fundamental Considerations in Language Testing.* Oxford: Oxford University Press.

Bazerman, C. (2004) 'Speech acts, genres, and activity systems: How texts organize activity and people', in C. Bazerman and P. Prior (eds), *What Writing Does and How it Does it: An Introduction to Analyzing Texts and Textual Practices.* Mahwah, NJ: Lawrence Erlbaum Associates (pp. 309–39).

Brown, H. D. (2000) *Principles of Language Learning and Teaching*, 4th edn. White Plains, NY: Pearson Education (Longman).

Brown, H. G. (2001) *Teaching by Principles: An Interactive Approach to Language Pedagogy*, 2nd edn. White Plains, NY: Pearson Education.

Brumfit, C. (ed.) (1984) *General English Syllabus Design.* Oxford: Pergamon Press, in association with the British Council.

Burns, A. (ed.) (2005) *Teaching English from a Global Perspective.* Alexandria, VA: TESOL.

Canale, M. (1983) 'From communicative competence to language pedagogy', in J. Richards and J. Schmidt (eds), *Language and Communication.* Harlow: Longman (pp. 2–27).

Canale, M. (1984) 'A communicative approach to language proficiency assessment in a minority setting', in C. Rivera (ed.), *Communicative Competence Approaches to Language Proficiency Assessment: Research and Application.* Clevedon: Multilingual Matters (pp. 107–22).

Canale, M. and Swain, M. (1980a) 'Theoretical bases of communicative approaches to second language teaching and testing', *Applied Linguistics*, 1 (1): 1–47.

Canale, M. and Swain, M. (1980b) *A Domain Description for Core FSL: Communication Skills.* Ontario: Ministry of Education.

Carter, R. (1997) *Investigating English Discourse: Language, Literacy and Literature.* Abingdon: Routledge.

Carter, R. and McRae, J. (eds) (1996) *Language, Literature and the Learner.* Harlow: Addison Wesley Longman.

Carter, R. and Nash, W. (1990) *Seeing Through Language: A Guide to Styles of English Writing*. Oxford: Basil Blackwell.

Chamot, A. U. and O'Malley, J. M. (1987) 'The cognitive academic learning approach: a bridge to the mainstream', *TESOL Quarterly*, 21 (2): 227–49.

Chomsky, N. (1965) *Aspects of the Theory of Syntax*. Cambridge, MA: MIT Press.

Coffin, C. (1997) 'Constructing and giving value to the past', in F. Christie and J. Martin (eds), *Genres and Institutions: Social Processes in the Workplace and the School*. London: Continuum (pp. 196–230).

Cope, W. and Kalantzis, M. (1993) *The Powers of Literacy: A Genre Approach to Teaching Writing*. London: Abingdon Press.

Council of Europe (2001) *Common European Framework of Reference for Languages: Learning, Teaching, Assessment*. Cambridge: Cambridge University Press.

EdSource (2008) *English Learners in California: What the Numbers Say*. Mountain View, CA: EdSource.

Evans, R. (1986) *Learning English Through Subject Areas: The Topic Approach to ESL*. Victoria: Curriculum Branch, Ministry of Education (Schools Division).

Evans, R. and Cleland, B. (no date) *The Topic Approach to E.S.L.* video, Victoria: Ministry of Education.

Halliday, M. A. K. (1975) *Learning How to Mean: Explorations in the Development of Language*. London: Edward Arnold.

Halliday, M. A. K. (2004) *An Introduction to Functional Grammar*, 3rd edn, revised by C. M. I. M. Matthiessen. London: Arnold.

Halliday, M. A. K. and Hasan, R. (1976) *Cohesion in English*. Harlow: Longman.

Halliday, M. A. K. and Matthiessen, C. M. I. M. (2000) *Construing Experience Through Meaning: A Language-based Approach to Cognition*. London: Continuum.

Howatt, A. P. R. with Widdowson, H. G. (2004) *A History of English Language Teaching*, 2nd edn. Oxford: Oxford University Press.

Hymes, D. (1972) 'On communicative competence', in J. B. Pride and J. Holmes (eds), *Sociolinguistics*. London: Penguin.

Hymes, D. (1977) *Foundations in Sociolinguistics: An Ethnographic Approach*. London: Tavistock Publications.

Hyon, S. (1996) 'Genre in three traditions: Implications for ESL', *TESOL Quarterly*, 30 (4): 693–722.

Language in the National Curriculum (1989–92) *LINC material available on CD ROM or DVD*, www.phon.ucl.ac.uk/home/dick/ec/linc.htm: LINC Project.

Leung, C. (2005) 'Convivial communication: Recontextualizing communicative competence', *International Journal of Applied Linguistics*, 15 (2): 119–44.

Leung, C. (2007) 'Integrating school-aged ESL learners into the mainstream curriculum', in J. Cummins and C. Davison (eds), *The International Handbook of English Language Teaching*. New York: Springer (pp. 249–69).

Leung, C. and Creese, A. (2008) 'Professional issues in working with ethno-linguistic difference: inclusive policy in practice', in D. E. Murray (ed.), *Planning Change, Changing Plans*. Ann Arbor, MI: University of Michigan Press (pp. 155–73).

National Curriculum Council (1991) *Circular Number 11: Linguistic Diversity and the National Curriculum*. York: NCC.

National Statistics (2007) *Schools and Pupils in England, January 2007 (Final)*. www. dcsf.gov.uk/rsgateway/DB/SFR/s000744/index.shtml, accessed 18 May 2009.

Office for Standards in Education (2008) *Schools & Inspection: Information and Guidance for Inspectors of Maintained Schools, Independent Schools and Teacher Education Providers*. London: OFSTED.

Qualifications and Curriculum Authority (2007) *The National Curriculum*. London: QCA.

Schleppegrell, M. J., Achugar, M. and Oteíza, T. (2004) 'The grammar of history: enhancing content-based instruction through a functional focus on language', *TESOL Quarterly*, 38 (1): 67–93.

Swales, J. (1990) *Genre Analysis: English in Academic and Research Settings*. Cambridge: Cambridge University Press.

Veel, R. (1997) 'Learning how to mean – scientifically speaking: apprenticeship into scientific discourse in the secondary school', in F. Christie and J. Martin (eds), *Genre and Institutions: Social Processes in the Workplace and School*. London: Continuum (pp. 161–95).

Widdowson, H. (1975) *Language as Communication*. Oxford: Oxford University Press.

Widdowson, H. (1978) *Learning Language as Communication*. Oxford: Oxford University Press.

2

Mainstream Participatory Approaches: From Slipstream to Mainstream

Frank Monaghan

From slipstream to mainstream

The arrival in the UK of Asian and West Indian families in the 1950s saw the gradual emergence of a variety of approaches to the teaching and learning of what we now in the UK term English as an Additional Language. Initially, provision for such children was heavily influenced by methods borrowed from the teaching of English as a Foreign or Second Language outside the UK with a focus on language structures and an aim of speedy assimilation so that the child should: 'become "invisible", a truly integrated member of the school community, sharing the traditional curriculum and participating in regular classes as soon as possible' (Derrick, 1977: 16, cited in Leung and Franson, 2001: 153).

June Derrick's wording is telling in its reflection of the tensions between participation and invisibility, sharing and integration, tensions that continuously appeared in official policy and guidance documents (for example SCAA, 1996; DfES, 2002) and have persisted through to today, as can be seen from this extract from *The New Arrivals Excellence Programme Guidance* (DCSF, 2007: 37):

> They need to have their bilingualism (and sometimes multilingualism) recognised as a positive part of their intellectual development and they need opportunities to use their home language to support their learning and development of English. It is important that they are made to feel part of the normal lessons and learning environment as soon as possible in order not to experience marginalisation and exclusion.

Their bilingualism is to be made 'visible' but only as a tool to support transition to English and access to 'normal lessons', rather than as an integral part of their identity and a positive contribution to diversity in the UK. The slim line between the promotion of diversity and the avoidance of exclusion has been a constant feature of official policy down the years and this has inevitably been reflected in approaches to teaching and learning.

In the early years and up to the early 1980s, provision tended to be through either full- or part-time English classes which took place in 'language centres' located either outside or within schools. In other words, the approach was premised on the idea that the 'problem' was with language rather than the curriculum and it resided in the students, who needed to acquire English as quickly as possible to 'fit in'. A typical approach developed in the late 1960s and in use in schools up until the early 1980s was the one enshrined in SCOPE (Schools Council Project in English for Immigrant Children, 1969), a series of booklets for use in withdrawal settings that provided a grammatically structured, topic-based course built squarely around the 'four skills' (reading, writing, speaking and listening). Of course, things were not quite that simple and even from the early 1970s on there were moves to a more integrated approach to meeting children's needs (linguistic and social) in the mainstream classroom.

In 1975, the Bullock Committee, of which June Derrick had been a member, produced its report into the teaching of English, *A Language for Life* (DES, 1975), which also looked into the needs of 'children of families of overseas origin' (at this time, approximately 3 per cent of children in schools had English as an additional language) and famously asserted that: 'No child should be expected to cast off the language and culture of the home as he crosses the school threshold, and the curriculum should reflect those aspects of his life' (§20.5).

This vision of a curriculum that might include rather than merely assimilate also took a seemingly less instrumental view of the role of the home language: 'Every school with pupils whose original language is not English should adopt a positive attitude to their bilingualism and wherever possible help maintain and deepen their knowledge of their mother-tongue' (§20.17). Equally, the learning of English was also regarded as integrative and continuous, rather than as providing a 'quick fix':

> the adjustment of immigrant children to their new environment and to learning elementary English is only the beginning of what for most is a long process. It is a process that consists primarily of learning to live in or between two cultures, and of learning to handle two languages or dialects. (§20.2)

The situatedness of learning, its *ecology* (Haugen, 1972), is at least partly acknowledged here, as is an important role for specialist language teachers who, it is recommended, should 'work in close liaison with other teachers in the school and should keep in touch with the child's education as a whole' (§20.10). The report also envisages a shift from a focus solely on language structures to a more genre-based approach (as one might expect from the report that sought to advance the concept of 'language across the curriculum') when it recommends that:

In the secondary school, pupils who are past the initial stage of learning English need help in coping with the linguistic demands made on them by the various specialist areas of the curriculum. To this end there should be close cooperation between subject teachers and language specialist. (§20.12)

This recommendation was part of a shift that grew ever more influential in the 1980s to what is termed 'mainstream' provision, whereby students are expected to learn English alongside and ideally through the content of the mainstream curriculum. This shift had both linguistic and political underpinnings. The former resulted from the growing influence of linguists such as Dell Hymes (1972) in the United States, who stressed the importance of communicative competence, and Michael Halliday (1978) in Australia, who was developing a genre-based approach to language development in schools. This was followed by highly influential work on second language acquisition that stressed its similarity to first language acquisition processes (Dulay et al., 1982; Krashen and Terrel, 1983; Krashen, 1985) which provided persuasive linguistic arguments for mixing English language learners with their target language peers. At the same time, there were growing concerns about racial segregation in UK schools, where numbers of students with English as an additional language had grown to approximately 7 per cent by 1983, culminating in the Swann Report, *Education for All: The Report of the Committee of Inquiry into the Education of Children from Ethnic Minority Groups* (DES, 1985), which regarded the existence of language centres as an example of 'institutional racism' (Chapter 7, 2.4) and recommended that 'The needs of learners of English as a second language should be met by provision within the mainstream school as part of a comprehensive programme of language education for all children' (Part V, 5.3).

This view was reiterated a year later in the Calderdale Report (CRE, 1986). It should be remembered that this was a period of considerable racial tension in the country, reflected in the racially motivated murder that year of Ahmed Iqbal Ullah in Burnage High School. The Burnage Report (Macdonald, 1989) provides a shocking catalogue of the blatant racism experienced by minority ethnic students at the hands of their peers, teachers and other adults in that school (and others) at the time. It was envisaged that the move into the mainstream, with its clear emphasis on inclusion, equal opportunities and full participation would help reverse this situation.

Pedagogic practices – putting theory into practice

This significant shift in policy began a process whereby second language acquisition became regarded, as Jill Bourne (1989: 64) put it, 'as part of a continuum of language development, not in itself a very different process from extending the repertoires of a first language across an increasingly differentiated range of domains'. In this conception, the needs of bilingual

Table 2.1 Teacher roles

Role	Description: The English language support teacher …	Setting
(a) Remedial	… provides individual attention to address perceived English language 'deficit', underachievement or 'social deficit'.	Mainstream or withdrawal
(b) Specialist	… draws on assumed understanding of second language development and classroom language use to intervene in pupils' language development or the language and learning environment to enhance pupil performance.	Mainstream or withdrawal
(c) Catalyst	… acts as a change agent for the classroom or curriculum, reappraising practice from equal opportunities and anti-racist perspectives.	Mainstream
(d) Good teacher	… is simply a good class teacher working co-operatively in a team structure to meet the language needs of all pupils. Mainstream and support roles may be temporary and interchangeable.	Mainstream

students are to be met within the mainstream classroom with the National Curriculum providing the content for the development of the required linguistic 'repertoires'.

Teacher roles

A model of 'partnership teaching' was developed in which English language support teachers worked together with their mainstream subject counterparts to ensure access to the curriculum. Following a survey of provision in six local education authorities, Bourne (1989: 107–8) identified four characteristic roles of English support staff, as shown in Table 2.1.

Bourne noted that role (a) was the most commonly observed, that few of the English language support teachers had any specialist language training and that such a role 'would not always seem the most effective use of a trained teacher's time' (1989: 108). In the introduction to their training materials on partnership teaching Bourne and McPake (1991) argued that the fundamental aim of partnership teaching was to develop a curriculum responsive to the language needs and abilities of all pupils, irrespective of whether they were bilingual or not, and this shift in focus from the linguistic needs of the individual bilingual child to more generalized notions of curriculum access, anti-racism and equal opportunities is reflected elsewhere in the literature and rapidly established itself as a new orthodoxy. For example, Josie Levine in her *Bilingual Learners and the Mainstream Curriculum* (1990: 277), argues that provision for bilingual learners must be intent upon:

Table 2.2   Categories and sub-categories of support

1 Direct pupil support	(a) In-class support	Obviating problems as they arise in a lesson.
	(b) Preparational support	To prepare the pupil for an ongoing lesson.
	(c) Remedial support	Pupils withdrawn for extra tuition.
2 Teacher/pupil support	(a) General class support	Team teaching in which the teachers' roles are ideally not distinguished.
	(b) Consultative support	To respond to immediate problems or to get ahead of potential problems.
	(c) Analytical support	To detect what might be going wrong in organization, preparation or in the learning process.
	(d) Observational	To observe a specific point in classroom organization, lesson preparation or the pupil's learning strategy.
	(e) Substitutional support	The support teacher takes over the teaching of a lesson.
	(f) Specific support	The follow-up to the analysis of a difficulty.
	(g) Specific withdrawal	For a short time span, as part of the general support strategy.
3 Support in curriculum delivery	(a) Planning support	Support in planning to identify potential pitfalls for pupils.
	(b) Material (preparation)	Help to make materials or make commonly used support materials accessible to certain pupils.
	(c) Curriculum support	Support to maintain the integrity of the curriculum for low attainers.

Integrating learning and language-learning.
Engendering self-confidence, and self and inter-group respect.
Being positive to pupils' identities and cultures.
Not 'selling short' any of the students.

Dyer (1988, in Biott, 1991) identified three main headings under which support can be considered and Biott further developed these into 13 sub-categories (1991: 8–9). In any given setting there is likely to be an unpredictable blend of these approaches with the admixture depending on the knowledge, skills, experiences and attitudes of the participants and level of commitment the institution brings to bear to enabling things to happen (for example, employing specialist, EAL-qualified teachers, building planning time into staff workloads, ensuring flexible grouping patterns to enable bilingual students to benefit from appropriate learning environments). Perhaps inevitably, given the multiplicity of roles available, the less clear foregrounding of linguistic issues, and the precedent of the status of 'other adults' working alongside subject specialist teachers (such as classroom assistants), it was common for the English language specialist to be seen by both their mainstream subject colleague and their students as the 'junior partner' in the relationship.

In her study of how power relations are played out in classrooms between English language and subject specialist teachers, Creese (2002) discovered that despite the rhetoric of equality of status, language specialist teachers typically occupy the role of 'facilitator' of learning whereas their subject specialist colleagues are positioned as the owners of subject expertise and this has a profound effect on how they both position themselves and are positioned by others. This extract from one of her classroom transcripts of conversations between students and teachers succinctly reflects the lived reality (2002: 605):

S1	Miss, what have you got that for [referring to the tape recorder]?
T	Because she [the researcher] wants to record what I am saying and what Miss Smith [the language specialist] is saying and then she can play it back and she can see if there is a difference between the two of us.
S1	There is.
S2	Yeah, I think there should be a difference.
T	Why?
S1	Miss, you're the better teacher, aren't you?
S2	Like if I don't understand and Miss Smith explains to me and I still don't understand and I call you over and you tell me a different thing.
T	So we see it from two different ways, you mean?
S1	But you're the proper teacher, aren't you?
T	Well, no. We are both proper teachers.
S1	She's like a help.

This supports similar findings found both in the UK (Leung, 2001) and elsewhere (Arkoudis, 2000). Nonetheless, these same writers have also discovered (albeit fewer) examples of more egalitarian practices leading to the sort of balanced provision for students (that is, a balance between meeting language development and curriculum access needs), as described by Gravelle (1996: 8): 'Bilingual Learners need both the curriculum that motivates and has relevance for them and the systematic language development and feedback that enables them to achieve within it.'

In order for this to pertain, teachers need that scarce commodity, time, in order to plan for the learning of their students and to decide who will take responsibility for which aspects of the teaching and assessment at any one time. In an idealized model of partnership teaching such divisions would be fluid, dynamic and ever-changing, with all roles available to both partners, but in practice it is likely that busy teachers will settle on workable compromises. Creese (2005) identifies ten modes of collaboration that range from the EAL teacher working alone in a withdrawal setting with targeted students, through the EAL teacher working inside the mainstream classroom on an ad hoc support basis with little or no joint-planning, to a full and equal partnership where both teachers take full responsibility for the learning of all students. No judgement should be made as to the efficacy of one mode over another (and Creese stresses that these modes are in any case not necessarily discrete but can and do frequently co-occur). That said, the 'support' role tends to leave EAL teachers positioned as somewhat peripheral figures who, while very possibly having a significant impact on their students' learning, have a lesser impact at the institutional level, as

Creese observes: 'generally, partnerships allow for language concerns to gain a more central place on school agendas, whereas support modes tend to limit EAL teachers' abilities to influence school policies and practices around the needs of linguistic minority pupils' (2005: 143).

What is also still missing from the equation is a shift in the curriculum itself so that it reflects the diversity in the classroom. This is important not merely to prevent students from feeling their prior experiences of life and learning are marginal, but also from a sociocultural perspective on education (Vygotsky, 1962; Bruner, 1975; Mercer, 2000) that requires teachers to assess and understand a student's current level of understanding in order to support their further development, something that is particularly important in the case of bilingual students (Cummins, 2001).

Learner role(s)

The 1967 Plowden Report, *Children and their Primary Schools* (DES, 1967), set the tone for the avowed child-centred view of education in UK schools when it famously stated that 'At the heart of the educational process lies the child' (Chapter 2, §9), and followed this up with: 'Individual differences between children of the same age are so great that any class, however homogeneous it seems, must always be treated as a body of children needing individual and different attention' (Chapter 2, §75a).

Again, the tension between the needs of the 'body of children' and the individual child has always been present in the busy mainstream classroom, especially within a culture dominated by a proscribed curriculum and high-stakes testing. In such a performance-driven environment it is perhaps not surprising that while the rhetoric of celebrating difference has been maintained, not much of a difference has actually been made. This applies perhaps most strikingly to the needs of bilingual children in relation to their first language. Despite Bullock's championing of the culture of home, the Swann Report famously consigned first language maintenance and development to the margins of the education system by describing it as 'best achieved within the minority communities rather than within mainstream schools' (DES, 1985: 406) and defining its prime role as being a 'resource to help with the transitional needs of a non-English speaking child starting school' (DES, 1985: 427). This attitude has been reflected in all government publications on bilingual learners since then, despite the growing research evidence on the role of the first language in cognitive development and attainment (Cummins, 1981; Campos and Keatinge, 1988; Lambert, 1990; Ramirez, 1992; Lucas and Katz, 1994). This 'transitional' attitude towards bilingualism, which might be characterized as 'it's just an awkward phase they're going through', is of a piece with the 'invisibility' strategy that has sometimes masqueraded as equal opportunities.

Recent initiatives, however, would suggest that the time is right for a reiteration of the distinctiveness of the bilingual learner, particularly in view of the 'personalization agenda' (DfES, 2006) and the recognition of the significance of 'assessment for learning' (Black et al., 2003) and its most recent articulation within the National Curriculum in the form of Assessing Pupils' Progress (APP) (DCSF, 2009). Personalized learning and teaching is defined as 'taking a highly structured and responsive approach to each child's and young person's learning, in order that all are able to progress, achieve and participate' (2009: 6). This could be regarded as no more than a virtuous exhortation, but the Standards website on personalized learning identifies five key principles relating to pupils that allow for a fresh approach in terms of mainstream participation (DCSF, 2008):

- They will be treated as partners in their learning, with joint responsibility for participating in the design of their learning.
- They will have their individual needs addressed, both in school and extending beyond the classroom and into the family and community.
- If they start to fall behind in their learning, they will be able to identify their weaknesses and how to improve, and will be given additional support to help them get back on track quickly.
- They will receive coordinated support to enable them to succeed to the full, whatever their talent or background.
- They will develop respect for others, self-esteem and skills for collaboration through learning in a mutually supportive environment.

So far little work has been done on this area with specific reference to bilingual learners, but it is difficult to see how these principles can be enacted in practice unless a holistic view of the bilingual learner is taken. They do provide some very rich opportunities and challenges.

The first two principles, for example, would appear to imply a more inclusive curriculum that takes account of children's prior knowledge and experience as a basis for future planning. This would have to include the role of their first language both in relation to their cognitive and their social development within and outside the school as well as their educational and cultural background.

The third principle raises the thorny issues of assessment and its purposes. Assessment for learning (which essentially involves using evidence and feedback to identify where an individual learner is in their development and what they need to do next to make progress) lies at the heart of the personalized learning agenda, with the Department for Children, Schools and Families (DCSF) allocating some £150 million between 2008 and 2011 on embedding it in schools. This should provide an initiative to take a more nuanced and varied approach to bilingual learners that takes account of their particular and distinctive learning pathway than is possible under the current arrangements of assessing them through the *Language in Common* framework (QCA, 2000). As Leung and Lewkowicz (2008: 314) succinctly put it: 'A key problem of assessment ... stems from ... benchmarking performances in relation to inadequate or inappropriate descriptors. In the mainstream education context, the problems arise from using first language descriptors for assessing second language performance.'

Following on from this, the fourth principle then poses the question as to what sort of additional support might be required by bilingual learners in order for their individual needs and talents to be fostered. This challenges the commonplace assumption that the mainstream classroom might always be the best (only?) place for bilingual learners to thrive as it is entirely imaginable (and was always envisaged as such by the original proponents of mainstreaming) that some of their needs might best be met through targeted and specific interventions around their English language development.

The fifth principle introduces another focus of personalized learning, which is on the benefits of group work and collaborative learning, which have long been key components of the mainstream approach, if not always successfully implemented. A new attention to the role of language in such encounters is likely to pay dividends for all, as evidenced by the work of researchers on dialogic teaching (Alexander, 2006; Mercer and Littleton, 2007). Care needs to be taken with the divide between rhetoric and practice in this area, however. The National Strategies envisage a more interactive approach to teaching and learning but the research evidence suggests that whole class teaching, in which teacher talk predominates, has actually become more entrenched (Mroz et al., 2000; Myhill, 2006) including, paradoxically, the use of so-called interactive whiteboard technology (Smith et al., 2006). Summarizing such research, Lyle points out (2008: 227):

> The dominant form of classroom practices emphasises whole class monologic interaction which constructs pupils as respondents only and limits their discourse. Such practices establish normative patterns of interaction which have been likened to a script followed by teacher and taught ... The privileging of adult voice displaces children's voices and limits their expectations of classroom discourse.

In their discussion of prevalent modes of teacher behaviour arising from the twin pressures of the Department for Children, Schools and Families' national 'Strategies' and high-stakes, league table-oriented testing regime, Solomon and Black (2008: 74) argue that 'the strong emphasis on ability and attainment in the current UK climate impacts on teachers' communicative behaviour and, consequently, on students' understanding of the learning process'.

It would seem we still have some way to go in personalizing learning and making the mainstream classroom a centre of participatory activity. A major reason for this, perhaps, is because there is as yet no specific EAL curriculum that teachers and learners can work within, leaving both unsure (as witnessed in the extract from Creese above) about how the additional language curriculum is to be developed, and, more tellingly even, what it might actually look like. It is to this we now turn.

The classroom as a site for language learning

In 1975, Michael Halliday identified the nub of the problem, writing of mathematics (though his comments could equally apply to any subject):

The core of the difficulty in the mathematics classroom is that the teacher often understands and takes for granted the whole register of mathematics, and thinks only of the mathematical aspects of these items, whereas for the learner they may also be unfamiliar language – they are 'peculiar' English. It is therefore desirable that the mathematics teacher should be aware of the register of mathematics as a sub-set of English. To this end, mathematics educators and English Language teachers should collaborate in the production of guidelines, illustrative descriptions and teaching materials concerned with this problem.

Over 30 years later that challenge has still to be met, not only in mathematics but across the curriculum. That said, considerable progress has been made, particularly over recent years and largely by people working within and further developing Halliday's systemic functional linguistic tradition in Australia and elsewhere. In this section I explore some of the insights they have produced and use examples from analyses from the teaching of history to examine how the 'peculiar English' of a particular register might be transformed into something students can learn to take for granted by becoming skilled users of such language.

Language at school has been described as the 'hidden curriculum' (Christie, 1985) as teachers and curriculum and assessment statements seldom make their expectations of language use explicit (Schleppegrell, 2004). This should not be surprising given how little attention is given to subject-specific registers (or indeed language in general) in most initial teacher education (ITE) despite the self-evident fact that 'language and content are never separate, that content in school contexts is always presented and assessed through language' (Schleppegrell et al., 2004: 68). In an effort to address this directly, various approaches such as CALLA (Cognitive Academic Language Learning Approach), CBI (Content-Based Instruction), CCLL (Content-Centred Language Learning), CLIL (Content and Language Integrated Learning), have been developed since the mid 1980s. What all these have in common is the recognition that schooling is fundamentally a linguistic process with students needing to be able (and to be enabled) to deploy linguistic resources that grow ever more complex alongside the increasing cognitive demands of ever-expanding specialized subject knowledge. In fact, a case can be made that it is the linguistic complexity of how ideas are expressed within subject disciplines rather than the nature of those ideas themselves that presents the greater source of difficulty for students. As Schleppegrell (2004: 2) argues: 'Students' difficulties in "reasoning", for example, may be due to their lack of familiarity with the linguistic properties of the language through which the reasoning is expected to be presented, rather than to the inherent difficulty of the cognitive processes involved.'

This is especially true of bilingual students, who may already be familiar with the concepts in their first language. Schleppegrell's analysis is based on a functional theory of language (in the Hallidayan tradition) that seeks to identify the ways in which linguistic features of a text are used to construct particular types of meanings.

School history provides a good example of this approach and the work of a number of scholars (Coffin, 1997, 2006; Veel and Coffin, 1997; Scleppegrell et al., 2004) are now drawn on to exemplify some of the insights that can and have been gained.

Reference has already been made to the 'hidden' nature of the language curriculum that is implicit in school subjects. The *Programme of Study* for National Curriculum History in the UK, for example, in a section headed 'Communicating about the past' (QCA, 2007: 114) states:

Pupils should be able to:

a. present and organise accounts and explanations about the past that are coherent, structured and substantiated, using chronological conventions and historical vocabulary
b. communicate their knowledge and understanding of history in a variety of ways, using chronological conventions and historical vocabulary.

The Explanatory Notes on this section (2007: 115) state that: 'Pupils develop writing, speaking and listening skills as they recall, select, classify and organise historical information, use historical terminology and language appropriately and accurately, and provide well-structured narratives, explanations and descriptions of the past.'

Only four examples of vocabulary of historical terminology are given (century, decade, AD and BC) but no advice whatsoever as to what might constitute 'well-structured narratives, explanations and descriptions of the past'. Teachers and examiners, obviously, do have expectations about these things and so success (or failure) may hinge upon a student's ability to display competencies they have had no opportunity to acquire through explicit instruction. In addition to the 'communication' strand, there are also other aspects of the curriculum that have linguistic implications. For example, students are expected to 'investigate, individually and as part of a team, specific historical questions or issues' (QCA, 2007: 114), which might involve not only reading and writing but also speaking and listening skills, including culturally specific knowledge of such things as turn-taking in conversation, how to disagree politely, how to fill in a form to join a library and so on. Bilingual students, like socio-economically deprived students, are less likely to be familiar with or have access outside of school to the resources that are part and parcel of such meaning-making and so can only benefit from explicit engagement with them.

In their discussion of the (Australian) New South Wales *History 7–10* syllabus, Veel and Coffin (1997: 191–2) argue that rather than representing a single genre, the language of history is better regarded as:

a wide range of genres, beginning with a variety which appears fairly close to ordinary everyday language use and extending through to a stage which is very far removed from such use, thus implicating other-than ordinary everyday social processes … this pattern means that students' ability to 'record', 'sequence', 'list', etc. has a privileged status earlier on in schooling, whereas the ability to 'make generalisations', 'determine cause and effect', 'develop a logical argument', etc. is privileged in later years.

They go on to analyse four texts (from a sample of 1,000) to identify the grammatical features that constitute the evolving complexity and abstraction students encounter (and will have to produce themselves) as they progress in the study of school history, starting with a relatively straightforward autobiographical account (the attack on Gallipoli) and ending with an evaluative exposition (the inequality of the United States–Australia relationship). Their analysis focuses on such features as increasing lexical density across the texts, greater use of grammatical metaphor, the shift from the personal to the institutional, and the expression of causality and temporality and their effects on the field, mode and tenor of each text, pointing out how these demarcate a shift from more 'everyday' spoken styles of language use to more abstract written forms. These privileged genres are also closer to the genres that are valued beyond the classroom and associated with power. They also discuss two competing pedagogical traditions within the teaching of history: the 'traditional' approach, with its emphasis on the grand narratives and logical analysis, versus the progressive approach, with its emphasis on personal response. This is significant because while the progressive approach opens up the classroom to the student voice, their prior experience requires the teacher to start from where the student is; it also runs the risk of leaving them there because it may not necessitate students acquiring the range of genres associated with more complex and valued meaning-making (Veel and Coffin, 1997: 198).

In a later study of the development of student writing in history from the same setting, Coffin (2006) reports that successful students are marked by their evolving use of grammar and technical vocabulary to express increasingly abstract interpretations of the past. She maps these developing genres to produce a table of key history genres (2006: 418).

The analysis of the genres shown in Table 2.3, accompanied by a detailed linguistic analysis of the students' writing, was then used as a basis for six days of professional development involving history teachers and researchers to devise approaches and units of work to embed the teaching of both writing and content. The 'teaching-learning' cycle approach that was adopted involved teachers using scaffolding techniques to enable the students to participate in ever new modes of discourse (Coffin, 2006: 424). The materials devised used historical content so that the language instruction they embodied was not seen as a distraction from the syllabus and teachers were persuaded of the value of paying explicit attention to the language demands of their curriculum. Another consequence was that there was a shift in teachers' use of language; they became much more explicit about the previously invisible aspects of history texts. From the student perspective, the study also found evidence of increasing control over the organization of their texts. Similar findings are reported in other studies of school history, such as Schleppegrell et al. (2004), and have been documented for other subjects (Christie and Martin,

Table 2.3   Key history genres

Genre family	Genre	Overall purpose	Structure (stages)
	Autobiographical recount	To retell the events of your own life	Orientation; Record of events (Reorientation)
	Biographical recount	To retell the events of a person's life	Orientation; Record of events (Evaluation of person)
Recording	Historical recount	To retell events in the past	Background; Record of events (Deduction)
	Historical account	To account for why events happened in a particular sequence	Background; Account of events (Deduction)
	Factorial explanation	To explain the reasons or factors that contribute to a particular outcome	Outcome; Factors; Reinforcement of factors
Explaining	Consequential explanation	To explain the effects or consequences of a situation	Input; Consequences; Reinforcement of consequences
	Exposition	To put forward a point of view or argument	Background; Thesis; Arguments; Reinforcement of thesis
Arguing	Discussion	To argue the case for two or more points of view about an issue	Background; Issue; Arguments/perspectives; position
	Challenge	To argue against a view	Background; Position challenged; Arguments; Anti-thesis

1997). Coffin concludes by pointing out that the collaboration between content teachers and language experts was a crucial element in the success of the project and this provides us with a model of what needs to be done to ensure the classroom is indeed a site for language (and content) learning. However, as Leung (2007: 253) points out, the integration of EAL students into the mainstream curriculum is 'an ideologically laden process'. As the discussion of the history of such provision outlined at the outset demonstrated, EAL has never been viewed simply, or even primarily, as purely a language issue, but rather as a contested and complex matrix of linguistic, social, cultural and political interests and imperatives. This has led to a situation where 'arguments emanating from other spheres of society often hold sway and policy decisions on ESL can be made on non-language education grounds' (2007: 253).

For some 30 years now, teachers and researchers have been rising to Halliday's challenge to 'collaborate in the production of guidelines, illustrative descriptions and teaching materials' – while necessary, this alone will not be sufficient to ensure real participation as this will also require larger and more fundamental changes in how such learners are to be truly included in/by the curriculum. This will crucially require the input and commitment of stakeholders outside the classroom too. As yet we can but hope that the mounting evidence pointed to in this chapter will finally hold sway over politicians and policy-makers so that bilingual learners can enjoy the best possible chance of effective participation in the mainstream classroom and so be equipped to make a meaningful contribution to the world beyond.

Points for reflection

1 What factors outside the classroom underpin the tensions between inclusion and assimilation reflected within it and what implications does this have in your view for the likelihood of this tension being resolved?
2 Bourne (1989) described second language acquisition as 'part of a continuum of language development'. What solutions and problems has this proposition led to in your view?
3 Gravelle (1996) argued that 'bilingual learners need both the curriculum that motivates and has relevance for them and the systematic language development and feedback that enables them to achieve within it'. What factors within and outside the classroom would you identify as supportive of and challenging to this view?
4 What opportunities and challenges does 'assessment for learning' pose for those working with bilingual students?
5 Genre-based approaches offer one way forward for systematic language and content teaching in the classroom. What implications does this approach have for the training of teachers?

Suggestions for further reading

A good deal of relevant reading material can be found on the following websites.

www.collaborativelearning.org
The Collaborative Learning Project supports a cooperative network of teaching professionals in developing and disseminating accessible teaching materials in all subject areas and for all ages. Lots of practical ideas and freely downloadable resources for teachers to use and contribute to.

www.mantrapublishing.com
Excellent range of high-quality dual and multilingual resources such as books, posters, friezes and signs.

www.naldic.org.uk
The website of the National Association for Language Development in the
Curriculum. Contains lots of information and links to other useful websites,
such as EMA services throughout the country.

Center for Applied Linguistics: www.cal.org

CILT (Centre for Information on Language Teaching): www.cilt.org.uk

CLIL (Content and Language Integrated Learning): http://ec.europa.eu.education/
policies/lang/teach/clil_en.html

Jim Cummins' ESL and Second Language Learning Web: http://iteachilearn.
com/cummins

European Bureau for Lesser-Used Languages: www.eblul.org

TESOL: www.tesol.org

References

Alexander, R. J. (2006) *Towards Dialogic Teaching*, 3rd edn. New York: Douglas.
Arkoudis, S. (2000) '"I have linguistic aims and linguistic content": ESL and
science teachers planning together', *Prospect*, 15 (1): 61–71.
Arkoudis, S. (2003) 'Teaching English as a second language in science classes:
Incommensurate epistemologies?', *Language and Education*, 17 (3): 161–73.
Biott, C. (1991) *Semi-detached Teachers: Building Support and Advisory
Relationships in Classrooms*. Abingdon: Falmer Press.
Black, P., Harrison, C., Lee, C., Marshall, B. and Wiliam, D. (2003) *Assessment
for Learning: Putting it into Practice*. Buckingham: Open University Press.
Blackledge, A. (2000) *Literacy, Power and Social Justice*. Stoke-on-Trent: Trentham
Books.
Bourne, J. (1989) *Moving into the Mainstream*. Windsor: NFER-Nelson.
Bourne, J. and McPake, J. (1991) *Partnership Teaching: Co-operative Teaching Strategies
for English Language Support in Multilingual Classrooms*. London: HMSO/DES.
Bruner, J. S. (1975) 'From communication to language: a psychological perspective',
Cognition, 2: 255–87.
Campos, J. and Keatinge, R. (1988) 'The Capinteria language minority student
experience: From theory, to practice, to success', in T. Skutnabb-Kangas and
J. Cummins (eds), *Minority Education: From Shame to Struggle*. Clevedon:
Multilingual Matters (pp. 299–308).
Christie, F. (1985) 'Language and schooling', in S. Tchudi (ed.), *Language,
Schooling and Society*. Upper Montclair, NJ: Boynton/Cook (pp. 21–40).
Christie, F. and Martin, J. R. (eds) (1997) *Genre and Institutions: Social Processes
in the Workplace and School*. London: Cassell.
Coffin, C. (1997) 'Constructing and giving value to the past: an investigation
into secondary school history', in F. Christie and J. R. Martin (eds), *Genre

and Institutions: Social Processes in the Workplace and School. London: Cassell (pp. 196–230).

Coffin, C. (2006) 'Learning the language of school history: the role of linguistics in mapping the writing demands of the secondary school curriculum', *Journal of Curriculum Studies*, 38 (4): 413–29.

CRE (1986) *Teaching English as a Second Language (The Calderdale Report)*. London: Commission for Racial Equality.

Creese, A. (2000) 'The role of language specialists in disciplinary teaching: In search of a subject?', *Journal of Multilingual and Multicultural Development*, 21 (6): 451–70.

Creese, A. (2002) 'The discursive construction of power in teacher partnerships: Language and subject specialists in mainstream schools', *TESOL Quarterly*, 36 (4): 595–616.

Creese, A. (2005) *Teacher Collaboration and Talk in Multilingual Classrooms*. Clevedon: Multilingual Matters.

Cummins, J. (1981) 'The role of primary language development in promoting educational success for language minority students', in California State Department of Education (ed.), *Schooling and Language Minority Students: A Theoretical Framework*. Los Angeles, CA: Evaluation, Dissemination and Assessment Center, California State University (pp. 3–49).

Cummins, J. (2001) *Negotiating Identities: Education for Empowerment in a Diverse Society*, 2nd edn. Los Angeles, CA: California Association for Bilingual Education.

De Courcy, M. (2002) *Learners' Experiences of Immersion Education: Case Studies of French and Chinese*. Clevedon: Multilingual Matters.

Department for Children, Schools and Families (2007) *New Arrivals Excellence Programme Guidance*. London: DCSF Publications.

Department for Children, Schools and Families (2008) *Personalised Learning*. www.standards.dfes.gov.uk/personalisedlearning/about/, accessed 16 January 2009.

Department for Children, Schools and Families (2009) *Assessing Pupils' Progress (APP)*. http://nationalstrategies.standards.dcsf.gov.uk/app, accessed 18 March 2009.

Department for Education and Skills (2002) *Removing the Barriers: Raising Achievement Levels for Minority Ethnic Pupils*. London: DfES Publications.

Department for Education and Skills (2006) *2020 Vision: Report of the Teaching and Learning in 2020 Review Group*. Nottingham: DfES Publications. http://publications.teachernet.gov.uk/eOrderingDownload/6856-DfES-Teaching%20and%20Learning.pdf, accessed 15 January 2009.

Derrick, J. (1977) *Language Needs of Minority Group Children*. Slough: NFER.

Department of Education and Science (1967) *Children and their Primary Schools* (The Plowden Report). London: HMSO. www.dg.dial.pipex.com/documents/plowden02.shtml, accessed 15 January 2009.

Department of Education and Science (1975) *A Language for Life* (The Bullock Report). London: HMSO. www.dg.dial.pipex.com/documents/docs1/bullock.shtml, accessed 15 January 2009.

Department of Education and Science (1985) *Education for All: The Report of the Committee of Inquiry into the Education of Children from Ethnic Minority Groups* (The Swann Report). London: HMSO. www.dg.dial.pipex.com/documents/docs3/swann.shtml, accessed 15 January 2009.

Dulay, H., Burt, M. and Krashen, S. (1982) *Language 2*. New York: Oxford University Press.

Edwards, V. (2009) *Learning to be Literate: Multilingual Perspectives*. Clevedon: Multilingual Matters.

Garcia, O. (2009) *Bilingual Education in the 21st Century: A Global Perspective*. Chichester: Wiley-Blackwell.

Gregory, E. (2008) *Learning to Read in a New Language: Making Sense of Words and Worlds*. London: Sage.

Gravelle, M. (1996) *Supporting Bilingual Learners in Schools*. Stoke-on-Trent: Trentham Books.

Halliday, M. A. K. (1975) 'Some aspects of sociolinguistics', in *Interactions Between Language and Mathematical Education*, Final Report of the Symposium sponsored by UNESCO, CEDO and ICMI, Nairobi, Kenya, 1–11 September 1974. UNESCO Report No. Ed-74/CONF 808. Paris: UNESCO.

Halliday, M. A. K. (1978) *Language as a Social Semiotic*. London: Edward Arnold.

Haugen, E. (1972) *The Ecology of Language*. Stanford, CA: Stanford University Press.

Hymes, D. (1972) 'On communicative competence', in J. B. Pride and J. Holmes (eds), *Sociolinguistics*. London: Penguin.

Kaufman, D. and Crandall, J. (eds) (2005) *Content-based Instruction in Primary and Secondary School Settings*. Alexandria, VA: TESOL.

Krashen, S. (1985) *The Input Hypothesis*. New York: Longman.

Krashen, S. and Terrel, T. (1983) *The Natural Approach*. Oxford: Pergamon Press.

Lambert, W. (1990) 'Persistent issues in bilingualism', in B. Harley et al. (eds), *The Development of Second Language Proficiency*. Cambridge: Cambridge University Press.

Leung, C. (2001) 'English as an additional language: Distinct language focus or diffused curriculum concerns', *Language and Education*, 15 (1): 33–55.

Leung, C. (2007) 'Integrating School-Aged ESL Learners into the Mainstream Curriculum', in J. Cummins and C. Davison (eds), *International Handbook of English Language Teaching*. New York: Springer International Handbooks of Education, Vol. 15. New York: Springer (pp. 249–69).

Leung, C. and Franson, C. (2001) 'England: ESL in the early days', in B. Mohan, C. Leung and C. Davison (eds), *English as a Second Language in the Mainstream: Teaching, Learning and Identity*. London: Longman.

Leung, C. and Lewkowicz, J. (2008) 'Assessing second/additional language of diverse populations', in E. Shohamy and N. H. Hornberger (eds), *Encyclopedia of Language and Education*, 2nd edn, Vol. 7: Language testing and assessment. New York: Springer Science/Business Media (pp. 301–17).

Levine, J. (1990) *Bilingual Learners and the Mainstream Curriculum*. Abingdon: Falmer Press.

Lucas, T. and Katz, A. (1994) 'Reframing the debate: The roles of native languages in English-only programs for language minority students', *TESOL Quarterly*, 28 (3): 537–62.

Lyle, S. (2008) 'Dialogic teaching: Discussing theoretical contexts and reviewing evidence from classroom practice', *Language and Education*, 22 (3): 222–40.

Macdonald, I. (1989) *Murder in the Playground* (The Burnage Report). London: Longsight Press.

Mercer, N. (2000) *Words and Minds: How We Use Language to Think Together*. Abingdon: Routledge.

Mercer, N. and Littleton, K. (2007) *Dialogue and the Development of Children's Thinking*. Abingdon: Routledge.

Mroz, M. A., Smith, F. and Hardman, F. (2000) 'The discourse of the literacy hour', *Cambridge Journal of Education*, 30 (3): 379–90.

Myhill, D. (2006) 'Talk, talk, talk: teaching and learning in whole class discourse', *Research Papers in Education*, 21: 19–41.

Qualifications and Curriculum Authority (2000) *A Language in Common: Assessing English as an Additional Language*. London: QCA.

Qualifications and Curriculum Authority (2007) *History: Programme of Study*. London: QCA. http://curriculum.qca.org.uk/uploads/QCA-07-3335-p_History3_tcm8-189.pdf?return=/key-stages-3-and-4/subjects/history/index.aspx, accessed 16 January 2009.

Ramirez, D. (1992) 'Executive summary', *Bilingual Research Journal*, 16: 1–62.

Schleppegrell, M. J. (2004) *The Language of Schooling*. Mahwah, NJ: Lawrence Erlbaum Associates.

Schleppegrell, M. J., Achugar, M. and Oteíza, T. (2004) 'The Grammar of History: Enhancing Content-Based Instruction through a Functional Focus on Language', *TESOL Quarterly*, 38 (1): 67–93.

School Curriculum and Assessment Authority (1996) *Teaching English as an Additional Language: A Framework for Policy*. London: SCAA.

Skutnabb-Kangas, T. and Cummins, J. (1988) *Minority Education: From Shame to Struggle*. Clevedon: Multilingual Matters.

Smith, F., Hardman, F. and Higgins, S. (2006) 'The impact of interactive whiteboards on teacher–student interaction in the national literacy and numeracy strategies', *British Education Research Journal*, 32: 437–51.

Solomon, Y. and Black, L. (2008) 'Talking to learn and learning to talk in the mathematics classroom', in N. Mercer and S. Hodgkinson (eds), *Exploring Talk in School*. London: Sage.

Veel, R. and Coffin, C. (1997) 'Learning to think like an historian: the language of secondary school History', in R. Hasan and G. Williams (eds), *Literacy in Society*. Harlow: Addison Wesley Longman (pp. 191–231).

Vygotsky, L. S. (1962) *Thought and Language*. Translated and edited by E. Hanfmann and G. Vakar. Cambridge, MA: MIT Press.

3

Beyond Key Words

Manny Vazquez

A 'making' moment

It's 3.40 p.m. and the end of the school day. A knock on the door of the EAL room and Bizhan, a boy in Year 11, announces himself, the usual smile and friendly greeting. The conversation goes roughly like this:

'Hi, Mr Vazquez ... I can't come to homework club, I'm making an exam tomorrow.'

'No, Bizhan, you're not making an exam tomorrow.'

'I am, Mr Vazquez, look, here is the paper.' He hands me the Statement of Entry. .... 'Tomorrow ... look.'

I put on my most serious face, look him square in the eyes, and repeat, 'Bizhan, I'm very sorry to tell you but you are not making an exam tomorrow.'

Mock agitation, a raised voice and an attempt at challenging me in a serious manner that Bizhan doesn't quite pull off, as he's had three and a half years of getting used to my sense of humour. I cut him short and say:

'Bizhan, you're not making an exam tomorrow ... you're *taking* an exam tomorrow.'

His face breaks into a wide grin, he slaps himself lightly on the cheek, laughs and repeats (with downward intonation, signalling acknowledgement of a lesson learned): 'I'm taking an exam tomorrow.'

As we were in an informal situation with five minutes to spare, I quickly pointed out on the board other verbs which go with 'exam' – '*pass ... fail ... retake ... sit*', and so on. The teaching point that I had in mind was related to the concept of collocation. Now this is something that the National Strategy for English and Literacy (in England, DfEE, 2001), which tends to concentrate on word–sentence–text level analysis, has not addressed. The National Strategy curriculum guidance is in effect an extension of the statutory national curriculum and it has been designed to shape both the content and the pedagogy for subject areas such literacy in English and numeracy in mathematics. I will return to collocation in English as an issue for EAL teaching and learning later.

Bizhan arrived from Iran in January of Year 8. He was literate, educated but was a complete beginner in English. He came to the Catholic boys' school where I've been teaching part time for a number of years. The school has very low pupil mobility in comparison to other schools with high EAL demands but every year we receive a few new arrivals at a very early stage of English fluency. Traditionally these pupils come from Eastern Europe (mainly Poland), South American countries and a sprinkling of Arabic speakers (from Iraq and Egypt). Because of the relatively low number of EAL mid-term admissions, EAL support within the school is able to provide sustained and long-term support to these students, effectively seeing them through from arrival to their public exams at age 16, and sometimes continuing on to post-16 work. But would anyone's expectation be that a pupil such as Bizhan should be making this kind of error in his speech (or writing) three and a half years on?

My aim in this chapter is to focus attention on an area that I believe is not receiving enough critical attention in our schools, particularly in relation to the kinds of learning goals we should be setting for pupils with English as an additional language. I would propose that given the way in which EAL teaching has been conceptualized in England over the last 20 years or so, we are (and continue to be) in danger of not adequately meeting the vocabulary learning needs of EAL pupils, and that this has direct implications for success in their public examinations and for their progression routes post-16. I will be providing some formal evidence for this claim further on in this chapter. I would, however, like to begin by relating two different examples of anecdotal evidence: the first takes the form of a private communication made to me by two colleagues who have never met, but both related the same occurrence taking place during a General Certificate of Secondary Education (GCSE) English paper; the second involves a pupil assessment I was asked to undertake in one of my local schools.

Anecdotes and research evidence

The case of Mona

During initial discussions relating to the focus for this chapter, a colleague with many years' experience at local and national level of working in this field told me how a few years ago during a public examination in a secondary school in her local area, many of the pupils had been thrown by the wording of one of the questions. The question represented a significant number of marks as the required response involved extended writing. The pupils were answering a question on Steinbeck's novel *Of Mice and Men*, a text studied in many upper secondary school English departments throughout England. The question itself asked pupils to display their understanding of a central theme in the novel – the dreams the central characters share, and how these dreams (in this instance) are not realized. However, the wording of the question asked the candidates to comment on the *futility* of dreams. This colleague reported that in that examination hall there were many pupils clearly troubled by the wording of that question, specifically because they were not sure of the meaning of the word 'futility'. This same event was also related to me by an assistant headteacher in a secondary school in my local area, claiming that it had caused significant distress to many pupils who, after the exam, felt that they had not dealt adequately enough with the question.[1] The stories were related to me approximately one year apart, by two teachers who have never been in communication with each other and who work in two very different parts of London serving a diverse spread of bilingual pupils. Were the implications of the use of the word 'futility' relevant to the candidates in only two schools in England in that year? I think not.

I also wear a second hat. As Deputy Head of Service I share responsibility for the EAL teachers across 14 secondary schools in West Town, a city borough located in west London. It is with my advisory role in mind that I'd like to relate to you my second anecdote, the story of a pupil I was asked to assess due to the concerns being expressed by her teachers. This pupil was no new arrival but a Year 13 student taking A levels. Like Bizhan, the issues raised by this pupil inform a wider concern I wish to address throughout the rest of this chapter.

Mona was a sixth-form pupil in a local Catholic girls' school. The headteacher had contacted me directly expressing concern regarding the pupil, who was now in the autumn term of her final year of study (Year 13). Mona had been in the school for just over four years, arriving at the start of Year 9 as an early stage learner of English from Italy. Although at the time of her joining there was no dedicated teacher of EAL in the school, Mona had a number of key elements in her favour: in terms of cultural, educational and religious ethos, there were clearly similarities between her schooling in Italy and her new school in London. The school itself had consistently drawn praise during government inspections (OFSTED), with the latest report in November 2006 ranking the school as 'outstanding'. A strong system of pastoral support, very good teaching and learning throughout the school and Mona's own background learning and prior knowledge were all important ingredients for her success in her GCSEs. However, six months prior to her taking the public examinations that would lead to gaining a place at university, alarm bells were ringing. The concerns expressed by her teachers centred around two areas: the first was the quality of her handwriting, and the difficulty teachers had of reading answers typically written under 'exam' conditions; the second was the organization of the writing itself, and its lack of structure when addressing specific questions.

Mona was without doubt a very bright and capable student. Her examination record, given her arrival as a beginner in English in Year 9, bore witness to this. At GCSE she had achieved English language C, mathematics B, science AAB, drama C, art A*, Spanish A* and last but not least an A* in Italian. She was currently taking A levels in mathematics, mechanics, physics and chemistry. I conducted an informal assessment, which comprised a 45-minute interview/discussion with Mona, and a reading test based on a Year 12 biology text which I (with a non-science background) could understand and use to see her ability to handle inference, anaphoric reference and embedded propositions, as well as her general understanding of the text.

Mona was very comfortable with being interviewed by me and did not see this as an intrusion or an unnecessary event. She was very aware that she had a difficulty, or 'barrier' (her word), which prevented her from writing appropriate answers to some questions under exam conditions. Her view was that in her written responses she would 'talk/think' *around* the questions, rather than shape an appropriate coherent response with the required logical pattern. She also said that there were times when she felt not completely secure with the meanings of subject-specific vocabulary, as well as with what she called 'ordinary' words. With regard to the two concerns expressed above by her teachers, Mona admitted she felt she found it difficult at times to express herself in writing, and that this made her nervous and affected her confidence.

In addition, throughout the interview Mona on several occasions put forward a view of herself as lacking self-esteem and of not being a 'good' learner. My response to this was emphatic; her date of arrival, academic record and current engagement with subject matter (studying A level maths, mechanics, etc.) all pointed to a very bright and able student with great potential.

My initial impressions and conclusions were these:

- Mona was a fluent reader. Many of the difficulties experienced by EAL learners with reading comprehension (such as back-referencing words, embedded meanings, etc.) did not seem to be a problem.
- When writing at her own pace, her handwriting was neat and definitely legible. It could be easily read by someone who was not used to her writing. (This observation was based on two examples she had in her folder, which she said were notes written prior to an exam.)
- Although she had obviously learned sufficient English to do well at GCSE, there was evidence (cited by Mona herself) of subject-specific vocabulary to which she had assigned only partial meanings. The example of 'polar'/ 'polarity' in both chemistry and physics was cited by her.
- Scientific language at this level of study, where abstract concepts are being explained, will of necessity involve the use of metaphor, simile and synonymous expressions, for example, 'Each atom is surrounded by four equidistant nearest neighbours.' Mona stated that she wasn't exactly sure what this sentence meant. I expressed surprise, and when I had taken a moment to check her understanding of 'equidistant' and the expression 'nearest neighbours' she immediately understood the full meaning behind the statement. I asked her if she felt that there were other occasions where she might be coming across examples where the net effect was one of partial understanding of the text or of a key task or question, to which she replied yes.
- Her poor handwriting under test conditions was related to a sense of panic or nervousness arising from partial comprehension of some key words or phrases. Her reaction was to write as much as she could related to the topic. In other words, in answering some questions it was highly likely that she was being 'topic' specific but not 'question' specific.

I suggested some strategies that both she and her teachers could try. There was much that Mona could do to help herself. By her own admission, she did not make use of either a general dictionary or specialist subject dictionaries. As I had discussed with her, it was essential that she get into a routine of listing any technical vocabulary she was unsure of, and looking this up in the specialist dictionary. She then needed to cross-reference the word to other specialist dictionaries and check the meaning there (for instance look up 'polar'/'polarity' in a chemistry dictionary and then also look it up in a physics dictionary). In addition, any phrases or words of what appeared to be 'ordinary' English of which she felt unsure also needed to be noted or marked with a highlighter pen. Mona then needed to check the meaning with peers or the teacher.

As to direct teacher help, I discussed the possibility with the head of physics of her working with Mona for some one-to-one sessions in which guidance for non-fiction writing could be offered. In short, this would be looking at examples of written answers, defining the conventions, modelling the thought processes, applying appropriate scaffolding and then practising independent writing. We agreed that two to three hours of dedicated, focused teaching spread out as a few short, 30-minute after-school sessions would probably be sufficient.

Mona went on to be successful in her A level exams. The above-mentioned strategies gave her the confidence and help to ultimately succeed. However, my belief is that the underlying problem that had triggered my involvement in the first place centred on a lack of sustained and planned vocabulary development on her part. Essentially there were gaps in Mona's knowledge of the target language (English), and these gaps were not just limited to technical language but centred more on her knowledge of collocation, idiom (literal versus metaphorical meanings) and knowledge of the 'general' vocabulary competent speakers of English take for granted.

One could draw an analogy comparing her language development to that of the building of a house from scratch: Mona's foundations (her prior learning and skills) were rock solid, and perfect for her to begin construction of her 'linguistic' house. In Cummins' (1996) terms she arrived with high CALP (Cognitive Academic Language Proficiency) in her first language, and also in terms of Cummins' interdependence hypothesis,[2] Mona probably engaged with the English educational system at the optimum time for her as a learner. All the rooms expected to comprise the house came together (the grammatical components), and the order of the rooms as one walks through the house (the syntax) flowed with a logical pattern. However, in each room of her 'house' there are gaps: the kitchen has its sink, and water flows from the taps, but one of the taps is missing. The kettle lacks a power cord. The large bay windows have curtains, but the curtains are the wrong size and only drop halfway down the panes.

When Mona arrived for the first time in a new country and had to learn not just a new language but also academic content through that new language, she could not have found herself in a more supportive environment than the school she went to. It was not the case that the school and the teachers did not want to help Mona. The question to ask rather is, was the learning environment able to pay sufficient attention to her language learning needs? Were the mainstream content learning lessons she negotiated throughout her time in school able to address the development of the kind of deep word knowledge a highly able student is likely to need as they progress on to more challenging, post-16 courses and more complex subject matter?

Developing vocabulary size

At around the time of my meeting with Mona, a paper by Cameron (2002) was raising similar issues to those I felt lay at the heart of Mona's difficulties. In her paper, Cameron looks at vocabulary size as one aspect of lexical development. The main data consists of vocabulary test scores of two groups of secondary school pupils in two schools, one Year 10 group and one Year 9. These two groups of pupils were mixed in terms of gender and language backgrounds. There were 96 English as first language speakers and 71 English as additional language speakers, a total of 167 pupils involved in the study. The majority of the EAL pupils were born in the UK or long-term residents, with eight of these having had less than five years of residence in the country.

The pupils' vocabulary sizes were measured in terms of the number of sample words they recognized in the various tests set at different levels of most frequent words: the first 1,000 words (1K), second 1,000 (2K) and so on. The tests used were the Levels tests. These tests were designed to give an estimate of vocabulary size for second language learners of general or academic English. The rationale for using these tests stems from an acceptance among researchers that vocabulary size is directly related to the ability to use English in various ways. Researchers working in this field agree that the 2,000-word level represents the most suitable limit for high frequency words, the classic list of these being Michael West's General Service List (for further discussion see Nation, 2001). Many of the words are function words such as a, *some*, *to*, *because*. The rest are content words such as nouns, adjectives and verbs (see www.rong-chang.com/gsl2000.htm or www.uefap.com/vocab/select/selfram.htm for the items on this vocabulary list).

Many older series of graded English as a Foreign Language (EFL) readers are based on these lists. It is important to note that the 2,000 high frequency words of English consist of some words with very high frequencies and some words that are only slightly more frequent than others not on the list. The first 1,000 words cover around 74 to 77 per cent of the running words in academic texts. Nation (2001) makes the all-important point that 'the high frequency words of the language are clearly so important that considerable time should be spent on them by teachers and learners ... high frequency words are so important that anything that teachers and learners do to make sure they are learned is worth doing'.

One of the key findings of Cameron's study was that there were significant differences in the scores at the 3K, 5K and 10K levels between English as first language and EAL pupils. Cameron (2002: 165–6) observes that:

The result indicates that EAL vocabulary development is not reaching the levels that might be expected, or that is needed by students for examinations and full social participation. The students in the sample had received 10 years of education in the UK through the medium of English, and yet the results show gaps in even the most frequent occurring words, and some serious problems at the 5K and 10K levels. Words at 3 to 5K are considered necessary for basic comprehension in English as a second language ... yet these students are one or two years from public examinations which require them, not just to understand basic texts, but to understand and produce precise accurate meanings in school and examination texts.

Schmitt et al. (2001) suggest that knowledge of around 3,000 words is the threshold that should allow learners to begin to read authentic texts, and that knowledge of the most frequent 5,000 words should provide enough vocabulary to enable learners to read authentic texts. Although many words may still be unknown, the 5K level should allow learners to infer the meaning of many of the new words from context, and to understand most of the communicative content of the text. Many of the students in Cameron's study had gaps at the 5K level. Given that the sample group were students who had gone through all of their education in England, what are the longer-tem implications for those students like Mona and Bizhan, who are much more recent arrivals?

Developing deep word knowledge

So far in this chapter there has been an assumption that the idea of what a word is, is generally a given or a shared notion. However, as Schmitt (2000) points out in his introduction in *Vocabulary in Language Teaching*, the term *word* is probably too general a term to encapsulate the many forms vocabulary can take. A good example of this is given by Schmitt when looking at the meaning of 'to die'. All of the following items are synonymous expressions within English, and are made up from one to four words:

Die
Expire
Pass away
Bite the dust
Kick the bucket
Give up the ghost

Clearly what we are now dealing with are concepts or ideas that are being expressed not just as individual lexical items but also as combinations of words; in the example above, most happen to be phrasal verbs and idioms. The reality facing language learners of English is that the potential knowledge that can be known about a word is actually a very rich and complex process. Nation and Nation (1990) propose the following list of the different kinds of knowledge that a person needs to master in order to know a word:

> The meaning(s) of the word
> The written form of the word
> The spoken form of the word
> The grammatical behaviour of the word
> The collocations of the word
> The register of the word
> The associations of the word
> The frequency of the word

How one goes about developing this deep word knowledge in EAL pupils within the context of how secondary schooling is organized is a very real challenge. One of Cameron's observations when trying to account for the gaps in vocabulary levels seen in the EAL pupils in her study gives cause for concern:

> Explanations for these gaps may lie in the nature of the learning environment for EAL and the possible lack of focused support it provides for vocabulary development. In the EAL situation, vocabulary coverage is not planned but arises from teaching in curriculum areas. Furthermore, intervention by mainstream subject teachers in vocabulary development may often be limited to simplification of unfamiliar words, rather than attending to the need to increase vocabulary size or to develop deep word knowledge. (Cameron, 2002: 67)

EAL – understanding pupil experience and language learning needs

The kinds of issues that can arise are well illustrated in the example below, which describes what happened in a lesson I was involved in. The teaching group was a Year 10 EAL Option. This means that EAL pupils in Year 9 have chosen EAL as one of their KS4 Options and in this particular case the focus of the work was additional support for GCSE English language and literature. Bizhan, the pupil mentioned at the start of this chapter, was part of this group. All of the pupils had arrived as mid-term arrivals in Years 7 or 8 with limited fluency in English, and the purpose of the option group was to ensure their attainment of at least a grade C in their English language GCSE. The class was looking at the debate around GM foods, and the final outcome was to be a discursive assignment around the pros and cons of genetically modified food. One of the many sources of information available, which was being used as a basis for whole class reading and discussion, was a BBC news web page with an overall title of 'Food under the microscope' and a sub-heading 'GM Food: a political hot potato'. The main text on the first page, which was used with the class, dealt with the issue around how the debate on GM foods had split both political opinion and the wider community. The text balanced the commercial advantages with concerns over health and environmental dangers. Vocabulary used, which was dealt with in class, were phrases like 'Frankenstein food', 'moratorium', 'commercial exploitation', 'opposition parties'.

The classroom discussion covered language issues, for example providing a gloss on vocabulary items that were likely to be unfamiliar to the pupils, and checking words such as 'moratorium' and 'regulating'. The phrase 'Frankenstein food' was not too problematic as 'Frankenstein' was a text used in the English department, so the associations made with GM foods were easy to make. The title 'A political hot potato' was also unpicked, first dealing with the idiom 'hot potato' and then extending the idea to the realm of politics and public and media perceptions. An unexpected issue, not planned for, arose that revolved around the government and political parties in general. The following two pages on the website centred on differing views between Labour and Conservative politicians. Although all of the pupils had been in the country for at least three and a half years and knew who the Prime Minister was, they could not name the leader of the Labour or Conservative parties (two largest political parties in the UK), nor had any knowledge of the adversarial culture of the House of Commons. The most telling point in terms of gaps in pupil knowledge, however, came at the end of the lesson and arose quite by chance; it was something I had completely missed. A chance remark from one of the pupils made me check their understanding of the title header 'Food under the microscope'. All, without exception, had taken this as a literal meaning, making (in their minds) the obvious connection between this title and the subject matter of food. None had applied the intended metaphorical meaning of this idiom to the learning context.

Virtually all of the students in this group achieved a grade C in their English language GCSE and went on to further academic study. They progressed, I would contend, however, with significant gaps in their knowledge of vocabulary and idiom. Just how these gaps can be addressed is not easy to resolve. The final lesson with this group at the very end of that autumn term was spent looking at the following billboard advertisement I had seen at a London Underground station, promoting a TV station and historical documentary programme: *Was the dodo a sitting duck?*

We had come to the end of the scheme of work in the previous lesson, and 50 minutes spent unpicking this advert proved an engaging and enjoyable task as a one-off lesson. Specifically, we looked at how two idioms had been effectively combined together ('dead as a dodo' and 'sitting duck'), the origin of the 'dodo' idiom, and how both linked to the advert, and we finished off with examples of both idioms in other contexts. The chance of having a 'spare' lesson at the end of the term had given an opportunity to develop some deep word knowledge in the students and they responded with enthusiasm and genuine interest. As an EAL teacher in a position, in this instance, to shape the learning outcomes for my group of students, it was very satisfying to know that the learners all left with a deeper understanding of these idioms and how they are a part of the 'cultural capital' many of us take for granted as fluent users of English. However, the deeper question for me as I left that lesson was, how does one accommodate the need for EAL students to develop this deep word knowledge within the way secondary schooling is currently organized?

To end at the beginning, when my student Bizhan insisted he was '*making an exam*', the error may (or may not) have been down to an issue around language transfer from Farsi into English. However, what is very clear for me is that this was an obvious example of where the language teaching model (that is, Bizhan's three and a half years of secondary schooling in England) is not sufficiently sensitive enough to ensure the development of even basic collocational phrases like the one cited. This question, and the ones that follow below, could form the basis for a widening discussion on whether current provision for EAL learners in state schooling is sufficiently attuned enough to develop vocabulary knowledge at both advanced and basic levels, particularly for those students seeking to progress with their academic studies post-16.

Points for reflection

1 What are the training, teaching and learning implications for mainstream teachers and their students if we want to ensure that learners can adequately engage with texts similar to the one on GM foods above?
2 If the 2,000 high frequency words are recognized as a critical and necessary goal in learning English, what organizational arrangements need to be made, particularly in English secondary state schools, to ensure that EAL pupils consolidate and know this group of words?
3 What are the implications for Continuing Professional Development programmes for teachers for developing the teaching of deep word knowledge in mainstream settings?
4 Particularly for those EAL learners seeking to continue their academic studies post-16, what opportunities do schools provide to ensure that students have consolidated their knowledge of the Academic Word List?

Suggestions for further reading

Bartels, N. (2009) 'Knowledge about language', in A. Burns and J. C. Richards (eds), *The Cambridge Guide to Second Language Teacher Education*. Cambridge: Cambridge University Press (pp. 125–34).
Schmitt, N. (2007) 'Current perspectives on vocabulary teaching and learning', in J. Cummins and C. Davison (eds), *International Handbook of English Language Teaching (Part 1)*. New York: Springer (pp. 827–42).

Notes

1 Private communication made to me by Margot Currie, Assistant Headteacher of Heston Community School, in November 2006.
2 The 'interdependence hypothesis' can be formally stated as follows: 'To the extent that instruction in Lx is effective in promoting proficiency in Lx, transfer of this proficiency to Ly will occur provided there is adequate exposure to Ly (either in school or environment) and adequate motivation to learn' (Cummins, 1996).

References

Cameron, L. (2002) 'Measuring vocabulary size in English as an additional language', *Language Teaching Research,* 6 (2): 145–73.

Cummins, J. (1996) *Negotiating Identities: Education for Empowerment in a Diverse Society.* California Association for Bilingual Education Ontario, CA.

DfEE (2001) *National Strategy Key Stage 3 Framework for Teaching English: Years 7, 8 and 9.* DfEE 0019/2001.

Nation, I. (2001) *Learning Vocabulary in Another Language.* Cambridge: Cambridge University Press.

Nation, I. and Nation, D. (1990) *Teaching and Learning Vocabulary.* Boston, MA: Heinle and Heinle.

Schmitt, N. (2000) *Vocabulary in Language Teaching.* Cambridge: Cambridge University Press.

Schmitt, N., Schmitt, D. and Clapham, C. (2001) 'Developing and exploring the behaviour of two new versions of the Vocabulary Levels Test', *Language Testing,* 18 (1): 55–8.

4

Connecting Communication, Curriculum and Second Language Literacy Development: Meeting the Needs of 'Low Literacy' EAL/ESL Learners

Alan Williams

Introduction: 'Low literacy' EAL/ESL learners in the educational mainstream

This chapter addresses working within a communicative paradigm to meet the needs of EAL/ESL learners who have low levels of literacy in their first language, and who usually have limited prior experience of schooling when they begin their learning of English as an additional language. As this chapter is describing practices in Australia, I will use the usual Australian terminology of 'ESL'.

When the teaching of ESL in schools is informed by a communicative approach to language teaching, the meanings learners deal with, and the ways in which they deal with them, are related to the requirements of the mainstream school curriculum. ESL support is directed towards supporting students for the demands that will be made of them across the curriculum in mainstream classrooms. Students become familiar with texts, vocabulary and grammatical structures relevant to their studies in mainstream subject areas, and are prepared for ways of encountering and using spoken and written language that will be expected in their mainstream classrooms. The ESL classroom prepares and supports them for the demands they will encounter across the curriculum. For students with age-equivalent experience of classrooms to their peers who are native speakers of English, this also means some adjustment to the prevailing expectations and practices of classrooms in English-speaking countries, which may vary to varying degrees from the expectations that apply in classrooms in the students' countries of origin.

In Australian public schools, while there is variation between states and territories, newly arrived ESL students receive six months' intensive ESL instruction, either in specialist centres or through additional support in their own schools. This entitlement is doubled for low literacy ESL students. In each state or territory there is an ESL component within the mainstream curriculum, which usually identifies low literacy learners as a group of students with particular needs, or as a preliminary stage of English language learning. Support is provided in ESL classes in schools, which are related to the ESL component of the relevant curriculum framework. These are concurrent with learning in other curriculum areas. In some schools, where there are concentrations of significant numbers of low literacy ESL students, there are more comprehensive transition programmes intended to support low literacy students across a more comprehensive range of curriculum areas.

In recent years global patterns of displacement of people and immigration have meant that traditional countries with high immigrant intakes have received more students from regions where literacy levels are relatively low, and civil unrest or war or long periods of transience in refugee camps (or combinations of all of these) have further limited educational opportunities. School-aged students arriving in English-speaking countries such as the UK, Australia, Canada and the USA are arriving in schools in need of ESL support but also having limited experience of formal schooling and little or no literacy in the students' first language(s). In Australia, this has added some new groups of ESL learners to school populations with an already diverse immigrant intake. Students with low levels of literacy have been arriving in Australian schools from areas of global conflict such as the Middle East (countries such as Afghanistan and Iraq), and the horn of Africa (countries such as Somalia, Sudan, Ethiopia and Eritrea). Many students among these have little or no literacy in their first or other languages, and many have little prior experience of formal schooling in their country, or in the countries in which they have lived while in transit.

When such students arrive in schools, ESL teachers and programmes face additional challenges beyond those faced by other ESL students with age-equivalent literacy in their first or other languages or age-equivalent schooling, in preparing these students for the challenges of mainstream classrooms, and supporting them in their learning. This chapter identifies the issues faced by such learners and their teachers, and briefly describes the strategies ESL teachers have developed to meet this challenge.

Before considering the strategies used to support these students it is important to understand their prior experiences and learning needs.

Low literacy ESL students and their learning needs

Different labels are used to identify these students in different countries. In Australia these students are now usually referred to as 'low literacy ESL students'. In the past, the term 'pre-literate students' was used, in an effort to signal that these had not yet had an opportunity to develop literacy skills, but this has fallen out of use in recent years. The arrival of these students has coincided with a period where there has been an increasing emphasis and focus on schools achieving high rates of success in teaching literacy in English, and increasing demands that schools prepare students for the expectations of work and life in a highly literate and technologically oriented society.

As with any label, terms that identify any group of learners contain a number of oversimplifications and overgeneralizations, and raise issues of definition. One such issue lies in definition and conceptualization of 'low literacy learner' as a category of need but also a transient category: when does a learner cease being a low literacy ESL student? Low literacy ESL students have reached middle to upper primary school levels or above, without having significant literacy skills in their home or other language(s); they have usually had little or no experience of formal schooling in their countries of origin. In some cases they may be part of families that have suffered separation and loss of family members, there may be family members experiencing post-traumatic stress, and in many cases parents and care-givers also have little or no experience of literacy or formal schooling.

These students face a mismatch between their socialization within disrupted and often predominantly pastoral or agricultural societies, and the expectations and assumptions that apply in formal education within the literacy- and technology-focused societies, such as Australia. In assisting these students in their learning in this context, while it is important to understand the nature of their learning needs and the type of support they require, it is also important to understand their circumstances, yet avoid falling into a deficit view of them as people, and understand that they are in circumstances where the skills and abilities they have already developed may be invisible or undervalued by the society they have moved into. The challenge for ESL teachers working with these students is to develop their language and literacy-related skills in addition to the usual language learning and cultural orientation needs of ESL students with age-equivalent education. 'Language and literacy skills' means the development of communicative capacity in spoken and written English, including both 'autonomous' and 'ideological' dimensions of literacy (Street, 1993). The 'usual language learning and cultural orientation needs of all ESL learners' relates particularly to the development of skills in using the academic language of formal schooling, and an ability to operate within the cultural context of Australian schools. This involves understanding more specific expectations of behaviour and approaches to study, and more general capacity to interpret stated and unstated expectations, combined with the development of a capacity to project an informed and credible bilingual identity in this context.

Starting points: the learning needs of low literacy ESL/EAL learners

Low literacy ESL learners share the usual learning needs of all ESL learners, in that they need to develop the capacity to use English in the ways expected by the school and beyond the school, and to access, explore and display their learning across the curriculum, as well as develop the range of age-appropriate language-related skills and understandings. This relates to interaction with their peers, teachers and other adults around and beyond the school. They need to develop their abilities to interpret and operate with the social and cultural milieu of the school and its community and the broader society.

The learning needs of low literacy learners diverge from those of their ESL student peers in three areas: language learning with limited literacy support, developing initial literacy in a second language, and socialization into formal schooling. While I have presented these as discrete areas, there are connections and overlaps between them.

The first is that as language learners, low literacy ESL learners do not have the age-appropriate first language literacy skills that ESL teachers are usually able to rely on to provide assistance for students in their learning of English. This means that students may not be so readily supported by written texts or written versions of spoken texts, nor can they use written language as a mnemonic, reading skills that usually aid recognition of words, give clues to the pronunciation of new words (even if these can be misleading in the early stages of second language learning) or help increase the variety or range of learning tasks students may complete in their language classes. There may be a small area of overlap with learners who are literate in a non roman script only, and who need to develop skills of recognition, production and the mechanics of the roman script utilized by English. But these needs are also not the same, in that students familiar with non-roman scripts can use their literacy to aid them in remembering or reflecting on their English language learning. Of course, as learners make progress with both their learning of English and the development of literacy skills, the extent of these differences diminishes.

The second area of divergence of need for low literacy learners lies in the socially framed requirement that English literacy is the priority of the school and skills need to be developed in the second or additional language before they can be developed in the learners' home language.[1] This means that learners differ from children developing literacy in their first language, when they can use their intuitive knowledge of spoken language as a foundation and connection for their development of understandings, skills and practices related to written texts. For learners developing initial literacy in an additional language their knowledge of the language system will be partial and limited, particularly in the early stages of learning, and so knowledge of words and sounds may not provide the clues they can provide to children developing first language literacy.

The third area lies in the need for these learners to be oriented and socialized into the expectations and practices of formal classrooms and schools. This relates to the social dimensions of the classroom, and expectations about behaviour, the nature of learning and what is valued in learning, the roles of learners and teachers and so on. This aspect of learning also involves the development of both learning to learn skills and frameworks of knowledge to support learning (such as knowledge that is considered so basic as to be assumed in mainstream classes. (See also Chapter 7, this volume.)

The first step: appreciating the nature of literacy

In socializing low literacy learners into English language literacy and formal learning, teachers need to work with an appreciation of the nature of literacy. It is beyond the scope of this chapter to explore or provide a comprehensive model of literacy in a modern technology-oriented society (see, for example, New London Group, 1996), but it is important to have a comprehensive appreciation of what is entailed in literacy. Street (1993) provides a two-dimensional model that provides a useful conceptual basis to guide teachers in considering what they need to teach and develop in their students. Street distinguishes the *autonomous* dimensions of literacy, by which he means skills and behaviours such as word recognition, decoding skills, spelling, writing skills, word-attack skills, the ability to look at a section of text and read what it says, and the ability to produce readable writing. These are the sorts of skills included in terms used by authorities such as UNESCO in referring to basic or functional literacy. The second dimension of literacy is labelled the *ideological*, and relates to the ways in which written texts are valued and regarded (the recognition of different types of texts and their significance), practices associated with texts, and ways of structuring and evaluating texts, and so on. These connect with broader aspects of the culture of English and may be culturally specific rather than universal.

The totality of these areas of learning covers the sorts of skills children living in English-speaking countries acquire over the years of preschool, early and middle primary years. These comprise 'scripts for schooling' and include the expectations that apply to classrooms and different types of tasks (including assessment tasks), understanding that underpins learning at later stages across disciplines, and aspects of literacy such as competence in interpreting and producing various types of texts used across the curriculum, and in the community outside the school. Gaps in this type of knowledge may be manifest when, for example, students are taken to be behaving inappropriately when undertaking tasks that may be new to them but very familiar to other students. It may also happen where students are prevented from making sense of a text because they lack the background knowledge assumed by the text, or when students demonstrate incapacity to undertake a simple task. One Australian ESL teacher observed 17-year-old recently arrived African students being unable to use a pencil and ruler to draw a straight line, as they didn't realize that the ruler needed to be held still while they moved the pencil (Hoban, no date).

The challenge for ESL teachers and their mainstream colleagues supporting low literacy students is to comprehensively address all of these areas, which result from many years of socialization into schooling for mainstream students. At the same time, there is the issue of how the school and ESL teachers can support the development of mother-tongue literacy. At present, in Australia, this is seen as the domain of first language community groups, and the school system and teachers are resourced to do little more than encourage their students and families to take up what opportunities for mother-tongue literacy learning might exist, and to value and appreciate the students' and families' use of the mother tongue where possible in school life.[2]

There are three levels on which adjustments can be made to support these students. At a *policy* or *programme level*, entitlements to ESL support can be adjusted to take account of the additional learning needs of these students, to give them extra time to receive specialist support, or provide support in different patterns from those given to other ESL students. At a *curriculum level* ESL curriculum documents can acknowledge these learners and their different prior learning experiences and needs, to identify their patterns of development and articulate their learning needs as they move through mainstream English-speaking schools, not only learning English but developing initial literacy in a language that is a second or additional language rather than their mother tongue. At the *classroom level* ESL teachers (and their informed mainstream peers) can use strategies and procedures that have proved to be effective in meeting the needs of these learners.

Supporting low literacy learners in ESL programmes

Policy or programme level strategies

The first step is for school systems, schools and teachers to identify the needs of low literacy ESL learners, and to organize ESL programmes so that these students can be adequately supported as they move into mainstream schooling. This involves:

- A sensitive initial interview and needs identification, which explores each student's literacy background and prior experience of schooling. This usually involves a first language conversation mapping the timeline of a student's experience of schooling, and discussion and demonstration of what literacy tasks a student can perform in their first language.
- The provision of adequate support in focused literacy-ESL classes. The support needed for low literacy students will be greater than for ESL students with age-equivalent literacy needs and second language literacy development. As literacy in the second language is usually also the student's initial literacy learning, more time is needed, and attention given to developing autonomous skills and understandings of the ideological dimensions of literacy, as discussed in the previous section.
- An acknowledgement that these learners will need more time than other ESL learners to adjust to mainstream classrooms and perform at levels equivalent to their peers, as their learning task is greater. This will mean receiving ESL support for a longer period of time, and closer monitoring of the development of their second language literacy skills as well as their second language and mainstream learning.

In Australia low literacy students usually have an entitlement to greater time in initial ESL support and orientation programmes; in some schools focused transition and support programmes are provided that are more extensive than those provided for other ESL students.

Acknowledging low literacy learners in the curriculum

Formal ESL curriculum frameworks need to acknowledge the particular learning needs of low literacy ESL learners and the nature of their development at different stages of schooling, so that administrators, ESL and mainstream teachers have explicit understandings of the circumstances and needs of these learners.

The presence of low literacy learners in ESL programmes has long been acknowledged in school systems in Australia, with ESL curriculum frameworks incorporating a 'literacy' stage that precedes the initial stages of ESL related to the age or stage of schooling of students (see, for example, the *ESL Companion to the Victorian Essential Learning Standards*, VCAA, 2008). While these stages identify simple literacy tasks, their positioning as 'preliminary' stages implies they are a prerequisite for language learning, rather than learning that is concurrent with the development of a range of English language skills. However, with increasing experience in supporting the needs of students, teachers and curriculum planners recognize that this is at best a partial understanding of these needs, which are more profound and longer lasting than presented by such a model. Instead, the effects of limited prior schooling are acknowledged as long term and gradually addressed over a longer period of exposure to mainstream schooling, extending to higher levels of schooling and higher ages. A student commencing schooling with low literacy at the age of 15 will require longer support than a low literacy student entering school at the age of 9.[3]

Formal recognition of the learning needs and progress of low literacy learners in curriculum documents gives legitimacy to both students and the progress they make, even though it is likely to be seen at times as limited or slow by comparison to more experienced learners or students whose socialization more closely matches the assumptions of the education system. It also legitimizes the additional and different work that ESL teachers may need to do with them.

Classroom strategies

At the classroom level, teachers use a range of strategies with low literacy ESL/EAL learners. This section provides a brief description of techniques used by teachers and the ways in which they contribute to meeting the needs of low literacy learners.

Connecting to the society at large and life beyond the classroom

Low literacy ESL students are not only adjusting to academic life in a new culture and country, they are also adjusting to the new society as a whole. As low literacy

ESL students have usually come from contexts where literacy is not widespread, and where technology is more traditional, they need assistance in understanding the nature of a highly literate, technology-oriented culture. This will involve teachers providing learning activities that include helping students explore common texts, such as advertisements, to understand their nature including their potential uses and the potential problems they can create; and helping them to understand and deal with the written language they will encounter in their environment, such as street signs, building signage, corporate logos and images, the way different media use written language, and how written language may interact with spoken language in contemporary English-speaking countries. While these needs will be strongest in the months immediately after arrival in the country, this area of learning is important, as low literacy students have not had the many years of immersion and socialization in the ways of a technology-driven society as have their peers who have grown up in such environments.

Connecting to the mainstream curriculum

Like all ESL students, low literacy learners need access to the mainstream curriculum. This means that ESL teachers have not only to assist in giving them access to aspects of the curriculum their mainstream classes are working on, but also to encourage the development of skills that will enable students to understand the teaching materials they encounter more independently and the work they are expected to produce. This obviously amounts to a significant task, across all areas of the curriculum, and involves the following:

- Familiarizing students with key areas of content knowledge and understanding, through the use of visual and other techniques used in content-based language teaching, so that students become aware of the content they are expected to deal with (see, for example, Kaufman and Crandall, 2005; Mohan et al., 2001).
- Checking and exploring knowledge that is assumed in the mainstream work low literacy learners are expected to be doing. For example, if students have to draw maps, or are learning about imperial expansion in the nineteenth century, knowledge of world geography and an understanding of the nature of a map may well be assumed and needs to be checked.
- Making students aware of language-based ways of representing such curricular knowledge and understanding, with explicit attention to and exploration of the sorts of books, writing, graphics, charts, maps, tables and ways of presenting knowledge.
- Making students aware of the sorts of activities and tasks they will be expected to undertake, and the expectations that apply to their performances in mainstream classrooms.

Undertaking such tasks involves explicit explanation, giving students the opportunity to react to what is presented to them, rather than lengthy explanations by teachers. Learning needs to be made concrete, and related to what students already know about and can do.

Socialization into the cultures of formal schooling and classrooms

Low literacy learners are likely to have limited prior experience of formal learning, even though they may have very well developed 'informal' learning strategies and skills. However, their lack of experience in classrooms may mean that they need to be helped to understand what is valued in that setting. This includes the obvious attention to expected norms of behaviour but also what is involved in the notion of being a 'student': what is considered as valued (and less valued) learning, ways of going about learning and demonstrating learning and skills. While much is related to curriculum requirements there are also less explicitly stated factors at play here, such as the ability to transfer learning to different situations and contexts, emphasis on learning how to learn, and expected and valued ways of presenting work. In the early stages this may be learning the rules for movement in and around the classroom, while after further progress it may involve an ability to understand what is expected in a given classroom task, and the ways in which teachers will assess and respond to students' work.

Language learning and the development of second language literacy

Low literacy learners need assistance with the acquisition of English in the same ways as all ESL students; they also need support in the development of literacy. Most learners of ESL are building their second language literacy onto the foundation of their first language literacy, a situation in which their existing literacy supports the development of their English language literacy. Low literacy learners face the challenge of not having first language literacy as a firm foundation for their second language literacy, as well as the further challenge of developing their initial literacy in a second language, without the intimate knowledge of the spoken language that usually assists the development of first language literacy.

Normal language learning activities

While many of the normal techniques used by ESL teachers are equally useful for low literacy learners, especially in relation to aspects of spoken language and the skills of listening and speaking, it is important that language is used and practised in meaningful contexts. These students tend to be more concrete learners in the earlier stages of their literacy development and may find abstractions about the language system difficult; they need to see how language is used in dealing with meanings in specific contexts and topics. However, because of their relative lack of literacy skills they will need additional assistance in using writing in tasks that support the language learning. In particular, teachers need to do the following:

- Provide clear models and examples of written language, and explicitly discuss and explain them so that students come to recognize different types of written texts and their uses.
- Explore how using writing can be used as an aid in assisting language learning, such as the use of personal dictionaries, labelling items to remember new vocabulary, and how writing down newly learned work can assist in remembering.
- Constantly make connections between written and spoken language (see below) in meaningful contexts, to show how what is said can be represented in written form.

Where writing is used in support of language learning teachers need to remember that a relative lack of fluency in writing might mean that an apparently simple writing task may lose its value if the writing dimension becomes the focus of the task, rather than writing as a support of other learning.

Developing skills and awareness of second language literacy

Teachers working with low literacy learners use a range of tasks that assist the development of literacy within the context of second language learning. The following sections illustrate some classroom tasks used by teachers in assisting the development of both *autonomous* and *ideological* dimensions of literacy.

Awareness of and fluency in autonomous dimensions of literacy

Being literate involves skills in the recognition and production of written language. Being literate involves fluency in these, as written language needs to be processed or produced in relatively short time frames and in ways that give a person credibility as someone who possesses literacy skills. Autonomous dimensions of literacy involve some 'top-down' skills related to predicting the nature and content of a text, and 'bottom-up' skills related to using and producing the detailed features of texts. The classroom tasks employed by teachers to engender these skills include the following:

- Word recognition tasks, such as recognizing words or phrases, using word search grids, labelling tasks, cloze tasks, crossword puzzles.
- Practice at copying texts to assist in the recognition of words, phrases and other features of written language, such as punctuation and layout; and to help develop and fine-tune precise motor skills involved in writing.

Sometimes practice at other classroom tasks such as colouring in, ruling lines and drawing shapes can also be useful here.

* 'Word attack skills' or strategies for 'decoding' an unfamiliar word or phrase, involving the development of phonic awareness and recognition of sounds within words and syllables.[4]
* Attention to the layout of texts, and different modes of visual representation often associated with texts, such as tables, diagrams, charts and illustrations.
* Attention to punctuation, layout and spelling.

Awareness of the ideological dimensions of literacy

Teachers of low literacy learners need to assist them to develop an apprecia-tion of the ways in which writing is used in conjunction with spoken English, and the significance (and often authority) attached to written texts and how this relates to spoken language. This means making students aware of the different uses of written texts, such as for enjoyment (storybooks, novels, comics), informative texts, and texts that may have additional force such as written instructions, agreements and so on. This involves exploration of different types of writing, how it is used and the expectations and conven-tions that may be involved. Classroom activities could include the following:

* Explicit discussion of text types, their uses and expectations associated with them.
* Explicit attention to and exploration of different features of different types of text.
* Comparison of different text types on the same topics, so students can see how the purpose and use of a text can result in different linguistic (or non-linguistic) features.
* Encouraging students to respond and react to texts, to evaluate them and reflect on how the texts they encounter can be of use to them.

Such tasks will help low literacy learners develop an awareness of both the differences between spoken and written language and the connections between them.

Connecting spoken and written language

Another aspect of second language literacy development that is important for low literacy learners (as it can be for other EAL/ESL learners) is the develop-ment of their understandings of the connections between spoken and written language, which might involve the following classroom activities:

* Classroom or other shared readings of written texts or stories.
* Students working with 'talking books' (following a tape or audio file containing a reading of the text the students are reading).

- Identifying on a written text what has been heard, such as choosing the word that was heard, or the part of a text where particular words, phrases or sounds are depicted.
- Dictations, including dictagloss, shared dictations and other class dictations.

Low literacy learners need to be given opportunities to explore such connections, in order to extend their knowledge of English and their awareness of the conventions of writing and how it relates to spoken language.

Other classroom strategies: the use of computer technology

Space prevents exploration of the many other aspects of classroom work that are of value for low literacy learners (such as the use of drama, art and music). However, the potential of computer-based technology is worthy of mention, because of the particular potential it offers for the support of low literacy learners. As with other ESL students, digital media, photos and sound files can be used as stimulus for discussion and writing tasks, while computer-based learning offers particular benefits for low literacy learners, beyond helping to familiarize them with the place of such technology in English language literacy. This lies in the potential that computer-generated writing has for assisting them to produce work that looks as accomplished as that of more experienced writers. The use of this technology has proved to be very motivating for low literacy learners in assisting them to produce written work.

Conclusion

The preceding section has identified some of the strategies and tasks ESL teachers can use with low literacy learners. While these strategies have been related to the type of learning they assist, an effective approach to supporting low literacy learners will involve integration of a range of tasks and activities around curriculum-related topics or themes, in which the point of focus varies between content, language, English language literacy and aspects of learning to learn. This needs to be done within a broadly communicative framework, related to the formal curriculum in which their learning will be evaluated. ESL teachers also need to be alert to the possibility that mainstream curricula may conflate several of the learning steps that low literacy learners need to make in order to demonstrate progress, and that their students are making progress not captured by mainstream curriculum frameworks.

Supporting low literacy students involves integrating learning on many dimensions associated with the mainstream curriculum, language and literacy. It involves additional time and care in checking assumptions, compared to the ways in which other ESL learners need support.

Points for reflection

1 How different is it developing an understanding of literacy and becoming adept in its practices in a language and culture that is not one's home language and culture, compared to the home language and culture?
2 How is learning a language different for learners who have little previous formal schooling?
3 What might be significant markers of progress for low literacy EAL/ESL learners? How might these be related to the mainstream curriculum, language learning and the development of literacy?
4 What is an appropriate term to use in identifying 'low literacy learners'? What are the advantages and disadvantages of the terms mentioned in the chapter, and what might be an appropriate term to use in your teaching context?
5 To what extent might issues of 'infantilization' arise in getting older learners to undertake tasks normally undertaken by younger learners, such as colouring in or the copying of writing? Why might such tasks be useful? How can these activities be set up in the ESL classroom so that such connotations are avoided?

Suggestions for further reading

Hamayan, E. (1994) 'Language development of low literacy students', in F. Genesee (ed.), *Educating Second Language Children: The Whole Child, the Whole Curriculum and the Whole Community.* Cambridge: Cambridge University Press (pp. 278–300).

Nicholas, H. and Williams, A. (2003) 'Oracy is more than the absence of literacy: changing learner groups in ESL classrooms in highly literate societies', in G. Wigglesworth (ed.), *The Kaleidoscope of Adult Second Language Learning: Learner, Teacher and Researcher Perspectives.* Sydney: NCELTR (pp. 29–52).

Notes

1 In Australia the development and maintenance of first language skills is often seen as the responsibility of the family or the immigrant community, rather than the school system. There is often a dearth of mother-tongue teachers who can be utilized in this task; there may not be concentrations of sufficient numbers of speakers of the same languages to enable this; and the pressures for speedy integration with mainstream education render such an approach difficult, if not impossible, in many contexts.
2 This often means encouraging and giving students opportunities to use their first language in school events, such as performances, the provision of multi-lingual signs around the school, translated newsletters and other modes of communication used by the school. Some schools have bilingual 'Multicultural education aides' to assist with communication between the school and the immigrant community.

3 This is the case if the student's needs are adequately addressed. Failure to recognize and address these needs adequately may result in a student requiring additional support for a longer period of time.

4 Second language learners may struggle with strongly phonically oriented approaches to teaching literacy in the second language as their understanding of the second language sound system is still emergent.

References

Hoban, P. (no date) Personal communication.

Kaufman, D. and Crandall, J. (2005) *Content-based Instruction in Primary and Secondary Settings*. Alexandria, VA: TESOL.

Mohan, B., Leung, C. and Davison, C. (eds) (2001) *English as a Second Language in the Mainstream: Teaching, Learning and Identity*. Harlow: Longman.

New London Group (1996) 'A pedagogy of multiliteracies: Designing social futures', *Harvard Educational Review*, 66 (1): 60–92.

Street, B. (1993) 'Introduction: The New Literacy Studies', in B. Street (ed.), *Cross-cultural Approaches to Literacy*. Cambridge: Cambridge University Press (pp. 1–21).

VCAA (2008) *The Structure of the ESL Companion to VELS*. http://vels.vcaa.vic. edu.au/support/esl/esl.html#structure, accessed 16 December 2008.

5

Teaching Approaches in Two-Teacher Classrooms

Angela Creese

Introduction

In a presentation at the recent National Association for Language Development in the Curriculum (NALDIC) annual conference, the keynote speaker, Pauline Gibbons, made an argument for looking at the kinds of *environments* that enhance learning. According to Gibbons, it's important to establish 'high challenge/high support classrooms which offer environments to intellectually challenge children or learners to do more than just reproduce the knowledge that other people have constructed' (2009: 5). She explicitly argues against 'simplifying' because such practices restrict what is available to be learned.

In her talk Gibbons gave examples of intellectually challenging approaches that occurred in a 'team-taught' classroom in which a science teacher and a specialist EAL teacher collaborated. Gibbons describes scaffolding as a means of creating high challenge/high support contexts. The concept is linked to the work of Vygotsky (1986) and involves, according to Gibbons, 'temporary help that assists a learner to move towards new concepts, levels of understanding and new languages … enabling a learner to know how to do something' (2009: 10). It provides assistance for learners to be independent by providing the skills necessary to face a similar context in the future successfully. Another term important in Gibbons' work is *message abundancy*, which she describes as learner opportunities to understand in different ways. 'So that you have more than one bite of the apple' and 'you don't just get told one thing once' (2009: 13). Here Gibbons is describing the need for an abundancy of messages which provide many opportunities to understand something. However, although such pedagogic strategies as scaffolding and message abundancy are crucial, she points out that it is teachers' assumptions and beliefs that are the major force behind the enabling and constraining effects of learning.

> For example, a teacher who sees knowledge as a commodity that is transmitted from the teacher to the students, is not going to be giving much airtime to listening to and building on students' ideas and prior

knowledge ... If you are a teacher who sees content as a body of something to cover, you're not likely to be thinking about the literacy demands in your subject. And if you see EAL learners as language deficient, you are unlikely to take the trouble to find out what a student knows in his or her first language ... So the way teachers think about these things actually impacts enormously on how they behave in the classroom and how they talk to students. (2009: 14)

In this chapter, I wish to explore the points raised by Gibbons in the passage above in the specific context of two-teacher classrooms in linguistically diverse secondary schools in London. Specifically, I investigate teacher beliefs and attitudes in relation to the pedagogic approaches of scaffolding, message abundancy, use of student prior learning and teacher-talk. I explore these through comparing the interactions (talk) of curriculum subject teachers (STs) and English as additional language teachers (EALTs) in the same classrooms working with individual learners of EAL. I also examine interview transcripts in which teachers and managers describe their beliefs about and attitude to EAL sensitive pedagogy for teaching EAL learners.

My overall argument is that the various pedagogical approaches taken by specialist EAL and curriculum subject staff have different values in schools, with the important work of scaffolding, message abundancy, teacher responsiveness and facilitation playing second fiddle to the transmission of subject curriculum. I also argue that within the curriculum-focused secondary school classroom, the pedagogies used by the EAL teacher are not viewed as similarly important and that this contributes to the low status of EAL specialist knowledge and marginalization of EAL learners further. The result is environments that are either 'high challenge, low support', where students are exposed to challenging curriculum content that is beyond their current level of comprehension in English, or, more frequently, 'low challenge, low support' environments (Gibbons, 2009: 5).

Teacher collaboration in England

Within the field of education we have been slow to investigate teaching beyond the normative model of the lone teacher working with his or her class. Discussions of pedagogy continue to conceptualize the classroom in terms of the one-teacher-one-class model. But this model does not do justice to the variety of teaching unisons and educational provision in our multilingual schools. Teaching unisons, whether in support or partnership mode, are a usual part of life in many primary and secondary UK schools. In fact, many of the key government reports speaking directly to issues of linguistic and ethnic diversity are built around developing such teaching partnerships. In England, teaching partnerships have had long-term policy support as an educational intervention in addressing the needs of young people learning

English as an additional language in school classrooms (DES, 1985; OFSTED, 2004; DfES, 2007).

Despite strong endorsement in policy documents, a recent report commissioned by a government agency appears to show few opportunities for teaching partnerships with schools presenting little evidence of partnership teaching (IOE, 2009). Several points are worth summarizing from the IOE report. First, today it is teaching assistants (TAs) rather than fully qualified teachers who are mostly engaged with EAL provision. In fact the title of 'EAL teacher' was rarely heard in the ten case study schools the research investigated. Moreover, the report found that the majority of TAs do not have training in EAL. Unsurprisingly, TAs had great difficulty influencing mainstream practice because of established staff hierarchies. The lack of specialist EAL teachers in schools had the effect of lowering the status of EAL knowledge, skills and support within schools. The report suggests that the rise in numbers of teaching assistants as opposed to specialist teachers leading on EAL further institutionalizes a pattern of lower status for subject EAL. Second, under school management structures, EAL was often embedded under Special Educational Needs (SEN) and learning support. The IOE report argues that this contributes to a lack of visibility and status for EAL and conflates the distinctions between EAL and SEN.

The dropping numbers of specialist EAL staff is described by both NALDIC (Davies, 2009) and IOE. NALDIC provides figures that show 12.5 per cent, or 1 in 8, of all pupils in English primary and secondary schools have a language other than English as their first language, with Panjabi, Urdu, Bengali, Gujarati, Somali, Polish, Arabic, Portuguese, Turkish and Tamil as some of the largest language groups represented. NALDIC points out that while the numbers of EAL pupils rose by approximately 23 per cent between 2004 and 2008, to 824,380, the number of specialist EAL teachers increased by only 8 per cent in the same period (Davies, 2009). As the IOE report points out, these figures show a mismatch between the demand in the education system and the available specialist teacher resources.

My own research makes a similar point (Creese, 2005a) regarding the lack of status in the education system for specialist teachers of EAL. However, I have also linked this discussion of EAL teacher status to wider hierarchies in education which rate pedagogies differently in classroom contexts. Ideologies circulate around different pedagogies, with pedagogies of transmission held in higher regard than other pedagogies because of an education system that is competitive and driven by particular kinds of assessments and final examination 'league tables'.

The research I describe in this chapter comes from a year-long ethnography in three London secondary schools. It involved working with 26 teachers. Of these, 12 were EAL teachers and 14 taught different subjects across the full curriculum. I collected audio recordings of classroom interactions, asking the subject and EAL teachers to wear portable audiotape recorders, and I conducted around 500 hours of open ethnographic observations and conducted semi-structured interviews.

Two-teacher classrooms in linguistically diverse schools

In this section I look at how these hierarchies are played out in the work of EALTs and STs. I present several data sources, which draw on interview data and recordings of teacher–pupil interactions in class. The first data set looks at two interactions and presents classroom transcripts of two teachers working in the same classroom with different students. The first transcript is the subject teacher working with an individual student learning EAL in a geography classroom. The second transcript is an EAL teacher working with a different EAL student in the same geography classroom. I analyse the two interactions with a view to understanding how question types and teacher responsiveness contribute to scaffolding and message abundancy for EAL learners. We know that teacher questions play a central role in classroom activity (Chaudron, 1988: 50). There are several schemes available to classify these question types. For example, Long and Sato (1983) have described the pedagogic possibilities of display and referential questions for second language learning with referential questions providing more opportunity for new information to be introduced and discussed. Tsui (1995) describes the various checks, requests and repetitions that teachers and learners use for clarification and in comprehending learning and teaching. Mehan (1979) outlines four types of questions that range from those providing restricted and highly controlled answers to those that require learners to generate procedures that will assist them in the future. These question types can be summarized as follows:

- *Choice questions,* which call upon the learners to agree or disagree with the teacher's statement and/or choose a yes or no response from a teacher list.
- *Product questions,* which ask the learners to provide a factual response such as a name or place.
- *Process questions,* which ask for the learners' opinions or interpretations.
- *Metaprocess questions,* which ask the learners to formulate the grounds for their reasoning, or to produce the rule or procedure by which they arrived at or remembered answers.

In addition to question types, I also consider how teacher responsiveness in the transcripts contributes to scaffolding and message abundancy. As Jarvis and Robinson argue (1997: 219):

> The teacher is responsive in the sense that through her minute-by-minute choice of contingent response to what pupils have said, she uses what the pupils say, and builds on it. Her response looks back to what the pupils have said, and forward to topic development or topic shift. In this process, fuller meanings are articulated, and alternative grammatical structures used.

The two extracts that follow come from two teachers working in the same geography class in the year prior to students' national GCSE examinations.[1] The EAL teacher has prioritized this class and has been encouraging the geography teacher to work with EAL students. However, despite these good intentions we will see that the two teachers find little opportunity or will to collaborate in the planning for language learning/awareness. The teachers are wearing a small microphone for data recording purposes and are moving around the class working with individual students. The class is made up of 50 per cent new-to-English 15-year-old students. This is a rather unusual scenario and reflected heavy migration from mainland Turkey at the time of data collection. Others in the class are bilingual and do not require EAL support, others are advanced learners of EAL, while others still are monolingual English speakers. The class is ethnically and linguistically diverse. The particular extracts below record two teachers working with two different newly arrived students. Neither of these two teachers speaks Turkish, the first language of the students they are working with. This reflects the typical arrangement in English schools where the majority of EAL teachers are not bilingual in a community language of the classroom. The geography topic is 'Climate/Seasons' and the students are learning to read and interpret graphs. The data were collected ethnographically (see Creese, 2005b). The data extracts represent typical exchanges between teachers and students in this class. In the extracts below the curriculum subject teacher is shown as ST, student(s) as S and the specialist EAL teacher as EALT.

Geography teacher working with student learning EAL

ST Join the dots to give a line graph. Join.
S Yeah.
ST Join with crosses. That is our line. It is our line graph. OK. Bars. This is a bar. A rectangle is a bar. These are all what we call a bar graph. OK. You done that? Now we have got to look at the climate. Look at this and think. Seasons are winter and summer. Yes? Seasons equals winter, spring, summer, autumn.
S Weather.
ST Weather, yes, it goes up and down. So it is a season. Winter, summer, spring. We have our winter holidays, summer holidays. In England. In Turkey, it is hot in summer and cold in winter?
S Yeah.
ST In the rainforests, it is?
S Cold in winter.
ST Is it cold? [Pause] It is hot all the time, isn't it? 26 degrees centigrade is hot, isn't it? We don't need sweaters and it is hot in January, February, March, April, May, June, every month. Every month it is high. 26, 27, it is always high. So we can say there is no seasons. The rainforests don't, do not, do not have seasons. We can write these sentences out. The temperatures, are they hot or are they cold?
S Hot?
ST Yeah. So we write this out. Write it on the paper. You can put the title, climate in Brazil. OK? (B5).

Even a brief analysis of this transcript shows that the ST asks a limited range of question types and is focused on curriculum transmission through making statements about the topic. The ST asks eight questions. Below I categorize these using Mehan's schema above.

Subject teacher: choice and display questions

1 You done that? (choice)
2 Yes? (choice)
3 It is hot in summer and cold in winter? (choice)
4 In the rainforest, it is? (choice)
5 Is it cold? (choice)
6 It is hot all the time, isn't it? (choice)
7 The temperatures, are they hot or are they cold? (choice)
8 OK? (choice)

All eight questions are choice and display questions in which the teacher is checking understanding of specific curriculum knowledge. That is, the teacher's questions require the student to display his or her understanding of the topic according to the teacher's agenda. All questions are formed so that the student need only give a one-word answer. The total range of possible answers to these questions is yes, no, hot, or cold. The geography teacher mostly appears focused on curriculum transmission. Some examples of this are:

- This is a bar.
- A rectangle is what we call a bar.
- These are what we call a bar graph.
- Seasons are winter and summer.

Also of interest is the use of the imperative to get the EAL to perform the task:

- Join the dots to give a line graph. Join.
- Join with crosses.
- Look at this and think.
- Write it on the paper.

Richardson Bruna (2007) argues that the use of the imperative in teacher–student interaction can position the student as incompetent. In the interaction above it appears to allow the teacher to give direct commands, which do not require further negotiation. Moje et al. (2004, quoted in Richardson Bruna, 2007: 254) call for 'school policies to reflect an understanding that learning for non-dominant students is more than just about acquiring content knowledge itself; it is about acquiring the ability to navigate and negotiate the oral and written texts of multiple discourse and knowledge communities'.

We now turn to look at an interaction in the same class between an EAL teacher and a different student.

EAL teacher working with EAL student

EALT   What you must do now, you need the book, we look at this. Now can you tell me, in summer, let's look at the questions here. The rainforests do or don't have seasons as we know them?

S	Don't.
EALT	What is a season, seasons?
S	[laughs as she tries to explain] Spring, summer.
EALT	Yeah, brilliant, great. OK. Temperatures are cool or hot all year round?
S	Hot.
EALT	We are not talking. Of course we are talking of Brazil now, yes?
S	Yes.
EALT	OK. You remember where Brazil is?
S	Hmm.
EALT	Good. Err, there is rain all month. Now what you have to do is, how much rain is there every year in England, in London?
S	80?
EALT	8, 80, this is?
S	[laughs] 800.
EALT	Thank you. Now what we have got to say is there is 800 millilitres of rain in London, how much rain is there in Brazil, do you know? How do you find out how much there is?
S	You have to look at the temperature.
EALT	Not temperature.
S	At the rain.
EALT	And what must you do to the rainfall?
S	You have to look.
EALT	What do you think you have to do to see how much there is for the whole year? This is how much rain there is in this month.
S	340.
EALT	And what month is that?
S	January.
EALT	So if you want to find out how much rain there is every month, what do you have to do?
S	You have to look at all these number.
EALT	Not look at all these numbers, what is the word that we say?
S	[not clear]
EALT	If you were to take 340, 360, what would you be doing?
S	Oh, times.
EALT	No, not times. What is that number, I mean symbol? It is not times, it is?
S	Add.
EALT	So you must add those numbers, OK? (B3)

Immediately we can see that the EALT asks many more questions than the ST. The EALT asks 19 questions and these include choice, product, process, metaprocess and display questions. These are:

1 The rainforests do or don't have seasons as we know them? (choice)
2 What is a season, seasons? (product)
3 Temperatures are cool or hot all year round? (choice)
4 Of course we are talking of Brazil now, yes? (choice)
5 You remember where Brazil is? (product)
6 How much rain is there every year in England, in London? (product)
7 8, 80, this is? (product)
8 How much rain is there in Brazil? (product)

 9 Do you know? (choice)

10 How do you find out how much there is? (process)

11 And what must you do to the rainfall? (process)

12 What do you think you have to do to see how much there is for the whole year? (metaprocess)

13 And what month is that? (product)

14 So if you want to find out how much rain there is every month, what do you have to do? (metaprocess)

15 What is the word that we say? (product)

16 If you were to take 340, 360, what would you be doing? (product)

17 What is that number, I mean symbol? (product)

18 It is not times, it is? (product)

19 OK? (choice)

Thus although all 19 questions are display questions they are much more varied than those shown in ST's extract. We see examples of choice, product, process and metaprocess questions. The last of these question types requires the student to articulate her thought processes. Clearly noticeable is how much longer the actual questions are and how much more grammatically complex they are. Also of note is that at least five of the questions are open and require the student to move beyond a one-word answer. In addition, there is a greater range of topics covered by the closed questions. Possible answers include: yes, no, hot, (number), (month), (mathematical symbol). Unlike the imperatives used by the subject teacher, the EAL teacher uses more interrogatives. Rather than transmitting facts to the student, the EAL teacher uses his questions to guide the student through the task. His questions are used to check comprehension of the key term 'season', to get the student to define a season, to establish that some places have constant temperatures, to check that the student understands the location of Brazil, to check that the student can read a graph/figure, to check knowledge of numbers in English and key mathematical symbols. This is achieved not through the declarative but building the narrative through questions.

In terms of scaffolding and message abundancy, we might argue that the EAL teacher is responding to the child's individual needs in a more nuanced way with more opportunities to extend and negotiate understanding around the themes of climate change and graph interpretation. Mercer makes the argument that 'To be effective, any teacher needs to explore the scope of a learner's existing knowledge' (1994: 10). This is achieved through eliciting knowledge from students, responding to what students say, and describing the classroom experiences that they share. That is, teachers need to follow a student's line of thinking in order to bring thinking on. At the core of this debate is an understanding of learning as dialogic. Teachers need to respond to what students say and vice versa. According to Brown and Wragg (1993: 22) in discursive terms, 'responding moves' are the linchpins of a lesson.

The interactional data presented above is reiterated in the interview data below. In the interviews the EALT and the ST describe the beliefs and values regarding their pedagogic roles in class. The transcripts show the contrast between the accessing and facilitation described by the EAL teacher and the transmission work done by the ST. First we look at how the EAL teacher describes his job.

> Well, first of all it is to assess the demands of a particular lesson in terms of language and in terms of the content, the concepts and see whether I can possibly get across a quite complex concept by simple means. (Graham, EAL teacher, Sinchester School)

The teacher speaks here of one of the core professional discourses associated with EAL work in the classroom: facilitation of learning. The teacher is concerned with accessing curriculum content by considering how it can be expressed in language that the bilingual/EAL children will be able to understand. Such work is often referred to as 'support work'. Implicit in this transcript is the notion of working out the child's level of understanding through scaffolded interaction. At the heart of this description are the ideas of recontextualization and reconstruction that Mercer describes (1994). The teacher aims to work with the child to elicit the knowledge they share. Also in the interview transcript we see reference to 'simplifying'. As described earlier, Gibbons sees 'simplification' as problematic. However, what the EAL teacher appears to be describing is modification rather than simplification. The EAL teacher is referring to the need to modify subject input so that students will be able to comprehend the message. As the earlier classroom transcript shows, he does this discursively through asking a range of questions on the same theme allowing the student to return to the subject matter and the concepts being presented more than once.

The subject teacher with whom he works constructs his role in very different terms:

> Well, I have expertise in terms of the curriculum, the syllabus and so I am directing what we are going to study next and plan that in relation to the curriculum. (Simon, geography teacher, Sinchester School)

In this teacher's professional discourse we see the importance given to the subject curriculum. The teacher has a 'directing' role, an overseeing role. The teacher is managing the subject content – what will be taught and in what sequence. He contrasts this with the following description of his partner teacher's EAL role.

> Graham is extremely good at just adapting, you will see him pick up a topic that you are doing. Write a few words, and photocopy it and come back with it. If there are two of us, I think it is a lot easier to achieve that aim [in class support] because you can help them [bilingual students] quicker. And also the support teacher will guide the weaker pupils a lot more and I will just be there for general queries but they will probably help the weaker child a lot more. (Simon, geography teacher, Sinchester School)

In this transcript we see the transmission of knowledge versus facilitation of learning argument constructed. The geography teacher describes his role as curriculum transmission and answering general questions. He does not view his work as involved with the one-to-one support work. He discursively removes himself from the particularities of one-to-one support. He very much constructs his role as dealing with the 'what' of the lesson. The 'how' of the lesson, in regard to bilingual/EAL students, is to be handled by the EAL teacher. For him support teaching is working with the few to facilitate learning. Moreover, he appears to conflate EAL with SEN as 'weak' and with those students needing the kind of one-to-one interaction that he positions the EAL teacher as providing. In the following extract we see the same ST describe the difficulties of subject delivery in his work with EAL pupils.

> They [EAL students] are just so demanding in terms of time, you either teach them or you don't and if you teach them nobody else gets a look-in, or the amount of time they have from me is so minimal that it is not fair on anybody ... Yes, I am always conscious that they want more time ... On the other hand you are aware that the lesson is coming to an end in five minutes' time, you want to do an overall summary for everybody and often it is much quicker to say well, that is the answer, and do it for them. (Simon, geography teacher, Sinchester School)

The teacher is stressing the importance of the whole-class plenary. The need to address 'the many' and to offer a summary of subject knowledge as well as provide answers to save time is a pressure that subject teachers report as common (see Creese, 2005a, 2006 for further discussion). The teacher clearly feels the pressure to deliver the curriculum. He needs to cover a certain amount of the syllabus and he recognizes that one way of doing this is to speak to the whole class. He also indicates that he understands that this kind of pedagogic delivery presents problems for him in meeting the needs of EAL students.

Explaining to EAL students takes more time. He wants to tell the students what they should know in terms of subject curriculum. He wants them to have the correct answers in order to pass their exams. His beliefs do not resonate easily with the need to engage in the kind of scaffolding and message abundancy work that Gibbons described earlier in creating high challenge/ high support classroom contexts. Nor do they chime with her view of the importance for all teachers of a focus on 'uncovering the subject' rather than 'covering content' (2009: 14).

We continue this theme of scaffolding and its pedagogic possibilities through investigating a different pair of teacher collaborators in a different London school. This pair of teachers is working in a Year 10 technology classroom in which the students are preparing for their GCSE examination. We have seen in the previous section how one EAL teacher asked many more questions than the ST he was working with. Below, we make a related point. We show a different EAL teacher again engaged in asking many questions while the collaborating ST is more willing to give out answers. In the following two extracts, the language and subject teachers are working with two different students on the same task. The first extract is the EAL teacher working with a bilingual student.

EAL teacher working with bilingual student – technology, Year 10

EALT   Right, what is the first thing you are going to do? Where is your design brief? Get your design brief. Good. Right, that is the first thing. Did you fulfil this? Did you do this? So the first things is [writes] did I fulfil ... Do you know that word? [reading 'The design brief'].

S   That means to complete it.

EALT   That's right. Did I actually fulfil it? Did I actually achieve it? Did I do it? That was your brief. Do you think you actually completed it?

S   Erm. No, because I haven't put the batteries in.

EALT   No, I mean the idea.

S   Yeah.

EALT   So, you can write a paragraph here, of what the design brief was, my design brief was to der der der der [writes]. What's the past tense of that?

S   'ed', is it?

EALT   Funnily enough! So you can ask yourself a series of questions, like on the board, look. So what went well out of this? Designing, the planning, the making and the evaluating. (Noreen, EAL teacher, Skonington School)

The EAL teacher here is attempting to get the student to complete the task by guiding them through what is expected of them. The pedagogic style is very much that of facilitator rather than transmitter. That is, she asks questions and encourages the student to arrive at an answer herself. However, the subject teacher in the same class adopts a rather different style of teaching.

Subject teacher and student (non-bilingual) – technology, Year 10

ST   You can also say how you got around this line here. You know, instead of colouring it in with black felt, you actually put metal around it, didn't you? That's an important point.

S   Yeah.

ST   You want to say how you did that. That is important. And you want to say about how you changed the size.

S   I didn't change the size.

ST   Yeah, you wanted to do it this big to start with and then you decided on this big.

S   Oh yeah. Do I have to do that as well?

ST   Yeah, put that down. Also put down about colour. You wanted it grey, but we didn't have any grey so you had to have it black.

S   Right.

ST   Get all those things down. (Oliver, technology teacher, Skonington School)

In these extracts the subject teacher gives more explicit instructions on what should be included in the finished piece of work. There are fewer questions and more direct guidance on what the student should write down. (A fuller explanation for this is given in Creese, 2005b.) The subject teacher and the EAL teacher are under different sets of pressures with the ST feeling the importance of transmitting the curriculum in both the whole-class plenary and one-to-one work while the EAL teacher appears to feel they have more time in the interaction offering more scope for message abundancy. In the last data set below we look at a deputy head speaking about teaching and working with EAL students. The transcript is long but worth producing in full for the number of issues it raises. I intend to pull out from this extract several themes that emerge from the way she describes the work of EAL teachers. The question the deputy head is responding to below is: *What is the role of the mother tongue in the mainstream classroom?*

Deputy head, Skonington School (from interview transcript)

1   It is a difficult one. And I think it is easier to see in terms of the kids. I think I can say it is so supportive for girls to have the opportunity to use their mother tongue for security and for understanding that I think it has a large role to play and we should never say, which is what I think we sometimes do say, 'speak in English, speak in English', as if it were better than speaking in Bengali, or Turkish or whatever the girls' mother tongue is and I think we should not discourage girls from continuing to use their mother tongue, I think it is important that they do so.

2   I think for staff it is more difficult to draw a line. Undoubtedly the use of the mother tongue for the bilingual teacher is very useful, particularly at early stages and if there happens to be a Turkish teacher and a Turkish girl then it is brilliant that they can use it. But I don't think that our support system for girls should be dependent on that because we are not all bilingual teachers, we are not multilingual anyway and we have girls, yes as it happens at the moment we have two Turkish-speaking teachers and a lot of girls who have just arrived for whom Turkish is their main language so it is convenient. But I think sometimes there is a danger of falling back on that and forgetting the other ways of accessing, of looking at the material of what is being done and making the English better and the English more accessible and relying a little too much on happening to speak the same first language as the girls.

3   I don't know, it is a bit waffly but I think it can be almost, it is wonderful as part of the support system for those girls and on occasions like the traumas we've had recently in the school around the racism allegations and all the stuff, and thank God we have got staff with whom the girls can feel that bit safer and that bit more confident and who can also act as interpreters, which is a total misuse of their time but it is good that we have got them.

4   But the philosophy of language development cannot be based on, can't be dependent on happening to have teachers who speak the first language of the girls, you know. Peter (non-bilingual EAL teacher) has got to be able to be just as successful as a support teacher and therefore the workings and the approach has to be based on the assumption that you won't happen to

speak their mother tongue but when you do, yes it can be a great support, it can be a great pastoral support.

5   I don't know whether sometimes it stays too much part of the classroom, I don't know. I mean this is vague observation, but whether sometimes a lesson is accessed by translation and I don't know whether that is terribly helpful ... And if the bilingual teacher is turned into a kind of interpreter sitting alongside of the pupil literally translating from one language to another as opposed to simplifying or something within English, but translating from one language to another then that is great because then the archaeology gets learnt but the English doesn't, yeah, and that's the risk. So a mixture, I suppose is what's right, but I think there is a bit of a risk in terms of too much use of mother tongue from teacher to pupil within the classroom. Outside the classroom, yes, for different purposes, but within the classroom it can be risky.

Like other participants within school communities, this deputy head is shown handling and making sense of the contradictory and ideological dilemmas she faces as her allegiances to different positions is continuously and temporarily reconciled and renegotiated (Billig et al., 1988). There is much I could comment on in this transcript: the different views of community languages as a resource, a right and a problem (Ruiz, 1984), all expressed with the same transcript; the construction of racism and the institutional work the bilingual teachers are asked to do around it (see Creese, 2004). However, I wish to focus now on one particular theme that emerges from the transcript: the power of different pedagogic approaches and the status the deputy head teacher assigns to them.

The deputy head makes an argument *against* the use of the first language beyond transitional pastoral support for curriculum learning. She argues that the support system for learning must be based on English. In particular she used the words and phrases '*accessing* the material' and 'making the English better and more *accessible*' (see paragraphs 2 and 5). These words can be traced back to earlier government reports, as indeed can references regarding the use of other languages as a minimal form of transitional bilingual support (DES, 1985). Indeed, as I have already indicated, EAL teachers themselves describe their own work in similar terms. Terms such as 'facilitation' and 'accessing' are key words in professional EAL discourse. One might think, then, that this is a clear example of professional and institutional discourses endorsing one another; that is, the facilitation of learning, the accessing of materials and the scaffolding of interaction are endorsed by the deputy head and the wider school community. However, quite the opposite is true. The endorsement of support work through English is only given such a favourable approval when set against support work in a community language. 'Simplifying or something within English' is preferred to 'literally translating from one language to another'. However, when English language medium 'support work' is lined up against whole class curriculum teaching it does not receive the same kind of endorsement. From the same deputy head comes the following comment.

> The job of EAL staff is to support the kids whose first language is not English at whatever level in the classroom. It is also to make resources more appropriate. This only happens on an ad hoc basis. There is a feeling that EAL staff have an easy life.

Unhappily this is not an isolated extract. Throughout my data there are instances of this kind of positioning of the work EAL teachers do in schools. Another example is given below from a different teacher in the same school.

> The support teacher doesn't have half these things to do – half their time is free – they haven't got reports to write, they haven't got to talk to parents, they haven't got this to do, they haven't got that to do – therefore they have got all that chunk of time you can occupy them with something else. I mean standing up in front of 20 to 30 children, delivering and teaching, is a very arduous job and I don't think anybody else does that sort of work, whether you be a support teacher or whether you be a headmaster. The nature of the job is very demanding. I think you just have to see support teaching as a different job. I think their role is totally different. They can work with a few kids who have special needs and problems and they can sort those through, which is not the same as teaching 30 children en masse hour after hour after hour. I mean that has got its demands. And it is not the same, it is a different job altogether. They get the same wage structure and things like that which perhaps they shouldn't, perhaps they should be seen as a separate entity, with different wage structures, different scales and things like that.

In this teacher's professional discourse we see the transmission of knowledge versus facilitation of learning argument reconstructed. This teacher presents the 'real work' as the teaching of the subject curriculum to the whole class and the responsibility that this places upon him in terms of exam results, school reports and contact with parents. Support teaching is working with the few to facilitate learning. In secondary school mainstream classrooms, subject teachers are associated with teaching the many, with transmitting specialized and specific content material and acting as gatekeepers to wider educational and societal successes. EAL teachers, on the other hand, are constructed as supporting the few and 'the needy' and as engaged in facilitation of learning rather than transmission of curriculum knowledge. Their knowledge base has become constructed as generic and non-specialized (Arkoudis, 2003; Creese, 2002; Lee, 1997) despite the educational benefits of the kind of work being done. The interactional analysis presented in this chapter has shown how different kinds of teacher–student talk present different kinds of learning opportunities. In the transcripts I have presented EAL teachers engaging in more scaffolding and providing more message abundancy than subject teachers and in doing so they create high challenge and high support learning contexts. However, these pedagogies continue to be seen as less important than pedagogies of transmission which address the many rather than the few.

Conclusion

Pedagogy is a complex social practice which draws in its participants in differing and complex ways. When two teachers work together collaboratively, classroom practices and knowledge take on a new complexity. Walkerdine (1987) has shown how pedagogic discourse constitutes the pedagogic subject and in doing so becomes not simply the message or the medium of knowledge but an instance of social construction. That is, the way teachers and other class participants speak and act will constitute classroom communities with their insiders and outsiders, winners and losers. Teachers' professional discourses are part of the complex web that makes up pedagogies. The importance of facilitating, accessing, scaffolding, providing opportunities for negotiation, for making form and function links, noticing gaps in the input and so on are all well documented in the psychology and English language teaching literature as facilitating curriculum learning and second language acquisition. However, in the mainstream classrooms in my study, these pedagogic skills were seen as remedial actions.

The owning of a curriculum subject or a clearly defined prepositional knowledge base with tradable expertise within the school appeared to be the basis of a 'proper teacher' status. There is a range of pedagogies at play in two-teacher classrooms with evidence of both pedagogies of transmission and facilitation used by different teachers. The analysis presented here highlights the importance of pedagogies of facilitation for students of EAL and the importance of time, questioning, scaffolding, message abundancy and negotiation for language and subject learning.

Points for reflection

1 How do teachers of subject curriculum and EAL use language in similar and different ways in interacting with students in the different teaching and learning contexts in your school?
2 Can you see evidence of how teacher beliefs and values shape learning and teaching interactions for learners of EAL? What might be done to change or enhance these?
3 What 'high challenge and high support' work goes on in classrooms in your school? What are the practices that create these contexts?

Suggestions for further reading

Conteh, J., Martin, P. and Robertson, L. H. (2007) *Multilingual Learning: Stories from Schools and Communities in Britain*. Stoke on Trent: Trentham Books.

Creese, A. (2005) *Teacher Collaboration and Talk in Multilingual Classrooms*. Clevedon: Multilingual Matters.

Denos, C., Toohey, K., Neilson, K. and Waterston, B. (2009) *Collaborative Research in Multilingual Classrooms*. Clevedon: Multilingual Matters.

Note

1 General Certificate of Secondary Education is the examination which 16-year-olds take in different curriculum subjects at the end of their 11th grade in secondary school in England and Wales.

References

Arkoudis, S. (2003) 'Teaching English as a second language in science classes: incommensurate epistemologies?', *Language and Education*, 17 (3): 161–73.

Billig, M., Condor, S., Edwards, D., Gane, M., Middleton, D. and Radley, A. (1988) *Ideological Dilemmas: A Social Psychology of Everyday Thinking*. London: Sage.

Brown, G. and Wragg, E. C. (1993) *Questioning*. Abingdon: Routledge.

Chaudron, C. (1988) *Second Language Classrooms*. Cambridge: Cambridge University Press.

Creese, A. (2002) 'The discursive construction of power in teacher partnerships: language and subject specialists in mainstream schools', *TESOL Quarterly*, 36 (4): 597–616.

Creese, A. (2004) 'Bilingual teachers in mainstream secondary school classrooms: using Turkish for curriculum learning', *International Journal of Bilingual Education and Bilingualism*, 7 (2 & 3): 189–203.

Creese, A. (2005a) 'Is this content-based language teaching?', *Linguistics and Education*, 16: 188–204.

Creese, A. (2005b) *Teacher Collaboration and Talk in Multilingual Classrooms*. Clevedon: Multilingual Matters.

Creese, A. (2006) 'Supporting talk? Partnership teachers in classrooms', *International Journal of Bilingual Education and Bilingualism*, 9 (4): 434–53.

Davies, N. (2009) 'View from the chair', *NALDIC Quarterly*, 6 (2): 3.

Department of Education and Science (DES) (1985) *Education for All: The Report of the Committee of Inquiry into the Education of Children from Ethnic Minority Groups* (The Swann Report). London: HMSO.

Department for Education and Skills (DfES) (2007) *Primary and Secondary National Strategies: Pedagogy and Personalisation*. London: DfES.

Gibbons, P. (2009) 'Challenging pedagogies: More than just good practice', *NALDIC Quarterly*, 6 (2): 4–14.

IOE (2009) *English as an Additional Language (EAL) Provision in Schools – 10 Case Studies*, Report produced by the Institute of Education under contract from the Training and Development Agency for Schools. www.teachingeal.org.uk/consultation.html, accessed May 2009.

Jarvis, J. and Robinson, M. (1997) 'Analysing educational discourse: an exploratory study of teacher response and support to pupils' learning', *Applied Linguistics*, 18 (2): 212–28.

Lee, A. (1997) 'Working together? Academic literacies, co-production and professional partnerships', *Literacy and Numeracy Studies*, 7: 65–82.

Long, M. and Sato, C. (1983) 'Classroom foreigner talk discourse: forms and functions of teachers' questions', in H. W. Seliger and M. H. Long (eds), *Classroom Oriented Research in Second Language Acquisition*. Rowley, MA: Newbury House.

Mehan, H. (1979) *Learning Lessons: Social Organization in the Classroom*. Cambridge, MA: Harvard University Press.

Mercer, N. (1994) 'Neo-Vygotskian theory and classroom education', in J. Maybin (ed.), *Language, Literacy and Learning in Educational Practice*. Clevedon, Avon: Multilingual Matters/Open University.

Moje, E. B., Ciechanowski, K. M., Kramer, K., Carrillo, R. and Collazo, T. (2004) 'Working toward third space in content area literacy: An examination of everyday funds of knowledge and discourse', *Reading Research Quarterly*, 39 (10): 38–70.

OFSTED (2004) *Managing the Ethnic Minority Achievement Grant: Good Practice in Primary Schools*, HMI 2072. London: OFSTED.

Richardson Bruna, K. (2007) 'Traveling tags: The informal literacies of Mexican newcomers in and out of the classroom', *Linguistics and Education*, 18: 232–57.

Ruiz, R. (1984) 'Orientations in language planning', *NABE Journal*, 8 (2): 15–34.

Tsui, A. B. M. (1995) *Introducing Classroom Interaction*. London: Penguin.

Vygotsky, L. (1986) *Thought and Language*. Translated and edited by A. Kozulin. Cambridge: MIT Press.

Walkerdine, V. (1987) 'Femininity as performance', *Oxford Review of Education*, 15 (3): 267–79.

6

Content-Language Integrated Approaches for Teachers of EAL Learners: Examples of Reciprocal Teaching

Candace Harper with Kimberly Cook and Carol K. James

Introduction

Although many EAL learners acquire English naturalistically through social inter-action, many also need support in developing the academic language skills required by the texts and tasks of school. EAL students often need *language-sensitive content instruction* to facilitate their conceptual learning through academic English.[1] They also need *content-based language instruction* to assist their development of the new language. Language-sensitive content instruction (also referred to as 'sheltered content instruction') refers to teaching in an academic content area using an array of instructional strategies to make the concepts more comprehensible for EAL learners (Faltis, 1993). Content-based language instruction refers to (language) teaching that is focused on language learning objectives but grounded in another curriculum area, such as history or science. Whereas language development is typically the main goal of content-based language teaching, subject matter learning is the central focus of the language-sensitive content classroom. In order to meet the learning demands of mainstream class-rooms, many EAL students need both language-sensitive content instruction and intensive, content-based English language instruction in the core curriculum.

Integrating language and content instruction has received significant atten-tion in the professional literature on English language teaching (for example Cantoni-Harvey, 1987; Chamot and O'Malley, 1994; Crandall, 1995; Kaufman and Crandall, 2005; Stoller, 2004). A number of definitions for integrated language and content instruction have been proposed; Davison and Williams'

(2001) description of content-based language teaching as a 'cline ranging from contextualized language teaching to language-conscious content teaching' (2001: 60) is an especially useful one. In this chapter we explore the notion of a continuum of emphasis on language development in integrated language and content instruction. When planning integrated language and content instruction for EAL learners, teachers need to consider the conceptual, linguistic and cultural challenges of the content area curriculum and the potential of their instruction. Emphasis on language development or content learning will also vary according to the distinctive linguistic and cultural needs and resources of their EAL students. A simple heuristic adapted from Harper and de Jong (2005) can (help) guide/inform this planning process, with the teacher asking the first of two pairs of questions:

> 1a. Do the concepts in the curriculum or the texts or tasks in your instruction assume background knowledge or require skills that some EAL students may lack and that can prevent them from learning?

Prerequisite knowledge and skill can include proficiency in oral language and literacy in English. It can also refer to social or cultural competence or the experiential and conceptual foundations for learning in school. For example, EAL newcomers to the USA may not have experienced any of the popular traditions of Halloween, such as telling ghost stories, going trick-or-treating, or carving a pumpkin (the process by which a jack-o-lantern – formerly called a pumpkin – is created and assumes a new name). They may not know the English word for ghost or other common Halloween icons or be able to recognize a picture of or identify objects associated with a witch – all familiar concepts to most school-age children who have been raised in the USA.

> 1b. If so, how can the linguistic, cultural and conceptual demands of the curriculum and your instruction be mediated so that all students have an opportunity to learn?

Teachers can address the second part of this question by using teaching strategies that are characteristic of language-sensitive content instruction. These include contextualizing instruction by making explicit links with familiar concepts and providing culturally relevant experiences, adapting texts by glossing or controlling unknown vocabulary, simplifying sentence structure, elaborating on implied logical relations to make inferences explicit, and using graphic organizers and other visual and non-verbal support for understanding key concepts in the content curriculum. An important but often overlooked resource in addressing this question is the large body of knowledge and experience that students bring to school. Helping them to make connections with and building on what they already know and can do will provide an important foundation for new learning. For example, relating the origins and traditions of Halloween with other cultural practices that are more familiar to EAL students (for instance the Day of the Dead, or La Toussaint) can help them to make sense of the new holiday customs.

In addition to dealing with the challenges of learning new concepts in a new language, many EAL students need help in developing oral language and literacy in English. Teachers can extend their instructional goals and target the academic language and communication skills that all students need to succeed in school. This shift in instructional focus requires that teachers ask a second pair of related questions:

2a. What aspects of linguistic and sociocultural competence are necessary for my EAL students to participate fully and equitably in school and society?

Addressing this question requires teachers to consider EAL students' distinctive oral language, literacy, social, and cultural needs in negotiating the content area learning demands of school and the complex process of developing social relationships with peers. EAL learners face issues of social isolation and cultural alienation on a daily basis, evidenced in seating and interaction patterns on the school bus, in the cafeteria, and in group work during classes (Duff, 2001; Olsen, 1997).

2b. How can I help them develop these aspects of academic, social and cultural competence in my classroom?

Addressing this question requires that teachers set objectives for English language and culture learning for their EAL students. The process includes identifying and teaching the grammar and discourse structures that students need to understand and communicate important ideas in the content areas. It also means identifying and teaching key words and phrases that EAL students will need to learn in addition to the technical, content-specific words that will be new to all students (Echevarria et al., 2004). It also means targeting the pragmatic skills that EAL students need to interact successfully across school contexts (such as different classroom conventions and varying teacher expectations) as well as in extracurricular settings.

These two sets of questions can serve as a basic planning tool for integrating language and content instruction. Teachers who ask the first set of questions acknowledge the ways in which linguistic and cultural diversity can influence learning in their classrooms. They attempt to overcome these cross-linguistic and cross-cultural barriers by adapting their curriculum and instruction for EAL students as well as for other diverse learners. However, teachers who also go on to address questions 2a and 2b understand that the linguistic and cultural dimensions of school often require explicit teaching and years of learning. They realize that comprehensible instruction is necessary but not sufficient, and their teaching is designed to help EAL students develop the conceptual knowledge and the linguistic, social and cultural skills they need to participate meaningfully and successfully in school.

Pedagogic practice

There is no single best approach to the complex process of integrating language and content instruction, and variations along a continuum of emphasis on language or content depend on the learners' variable needs and strengths and on other contextual factors. We provide two classroom examples to illustrate how two teachers[2] adapted and implemented a particular pedagogical structure – reciprocal teaching – in different ways, and how their classrooms are situated with respect to an emphasis on content or on language (toward, language-sensitive *content* teaching or towards content-based *language* teaching).

Reciprocal teaching

Reciprocal teaching (RT) is an instructional technique using a set of reading strategies in small group discussions of texts. Palincsar and Brown (1984) initially developed RT for fluent English-speaking students in the middle grades who could decode text but had difficulty in reading with comprehension. Palincsar and Brown believed that students could become better readers by practising and internalizing strategies used by good readers. In their original model, a group of between four and seven students read sections of text and practised four reading strategies: predicting, questioning, summarizing, and clarifying. A single student was designated to lead discussion on each section of text by applying these four strategies. This role then passed to another student as the group continued on to the next section of text. Reciprocal teaching has been implemented in a number of different classroom settings, and adaptations to RT have proven beneficial for a wider range of students than Palincsar and Brown originally intended (Marks et al., 1993; see also Rosenshine and Meister, 1994, for a review of these early studies).

In the two classes featured here, the teachers' modifications to the RT instructional roles and routines reflect their different emphases on language and content learning. Following a brief description of each teacher's modification and implementation of RT, we analyse the integration of language and content instruction in each class by applying the two sets of questions presented above to understand their different positions along this hypothetical continuum. Finally, we discuss several limitations and future implications of integrating language and content instruction for EAL students. In Appendix 6.1 we provide a table comparing the features of the original RT model with the two teachers' RT adaptations.

Adapting and implementing RT in Carla's class

The first example is a mainstream 3rd grade science class in a primary school with a large enrolment of students from mixed linguistic, ethnic, racial and socioeconomic backgrounds. EAL learners at each grade level are clustered and assigned to one or more classes in which the teachers have received some professional development on how to work effectively with EAL students. With a graduate diploma in teaching EAL and more than 20 years of primary teaching experience, Carla has more EAL preparation than most of her colleagues. This year, six of the 15 students in her 3rd grade class are EAL learners from different language backgrounds. Their oral English ability levels range from beginner to advanced, and although several have basic literacy skills in their native language, all are below grade level in their ability to read and write in English. Most of Carla's English-proficient students are just beginning to read difficult texts, and the 3rd grade curriculum requires that students read to learn from content area textbooks. Because earlier research had found that RT was most effective with students like Carla's who had good decoding skills but limited reading comprehension, she decided to introduce RT in her science class using the grade-level science textbook. She planned to build on her students' basic reading skills and develop their ability to understand what they read, and to learn key concepts and new vocabulary through reading. Carla implemented RT twice each week during the 40-minute science period. She modified the strategies and the process used in the original RT model by increasing opportunities for her students to build background knowledge and contextualize the readings. She also increased the support they needed to engage in meaningful conversations about what they were reading and to learn new words in the context of these readings. All of these instructional practices have been documented as effective language and literacy instruction for EAL students (Freeman and Freeman, 2000; Pica, 1994; Swain and Lapkin, 1998).

Contextualizing the reading

Preparing her students to use RT successfully did not happen overnight. Throughout the school year Carla used a series of techniques to support the RT process, including modelling, demonstrating, and monitoring their use of strategies. In addition, because she knew that many of the concepts in the science curriculum would be unfamiliar to her students, Carla began each new chapter with an experience-based activity such as walking through a nearby nature area, setting up a hands-on experiment, or observing and recording empirical data. These activities were designed to activate and develop students' background knowledge, contextualize the readings, and increase opportunities for them to make connections with and participate meaningfully in related discussions of the text.

These pre-reading activities were also motivating for Carla's students. Student engagement with a topic prior to reading goes a long way in mediating the difficulty of content area texts. In a technique she calls 'teaching the text backwards' Jameson (1998) explains that engaging students in extension and enrichment activities, and discussing the questions that typically follow the reading in a traditional textbook *prior* to reading the text, helps to introduce important vocabulary and ground key concepts in meaningful experience. This 'frontloading' of reading is helpful for many students, but it is essential for EAL learners, who may lack the assumed foundational knowledge needed for learning new concepts through a new language.

Communicating in small groups

Carla emphasized the importance of collaborative group work in all of her classes, but she felt that the success of RT depended largely on her students' ability to work meaningfully and cohesively with their peers. To participate effectively in cooperative group work, students must be able to communicate using social and academic discourse functions such as listening carefully, taking turns to speak, proposing and negotiating differences of opinion, and providing constructive feedback in positive ways. Collaborative discourse is especially important in creating and maintaining a motivating and supportive environment for RT group work. For Carla's EAL students, her attention to the social and functional role of language provided them with the practice they needed to use the appropriate spoken language conventions that allowed them to integrate socially and to contribute and learn in the RT groups. Carla believed that it was essential to take the extra time to set expectations for cooperative behaviour early and to model and practise *before* the small group RT sessions began as well as throughout the school year. She occasionally videotaped the RT sessions and she regularly used notes from her personal observations in class to identify specific examples of cooperative behaviour and to acknowledge students individually. She found that attention to the process and sharing these successes motivated her students to work collaboratively.

Learning new vocabulary

Understanding the meaning of words is essential in reading to learn, and most EAL learners find that vocabulary is a barrier to reading in a new language. Much of the linguistic load of the science curriculum lies in the large number of new words, and while the academic vocabulary encountered in Carla's science class was difficult for many of her students, it was especially challenging for her EAL students. Carla used RT strategies to help students uncover the meanings of new words in context, and to clarify and discuss meaning in relation to form and spelling. Through the RT group discussions, key words were repeated frequently and defined in multiple ways. For Carla's EAL students, this repetition and focus on the meaning of key content words provided multiple points of access to their meaning and served as valuable opportunities for both vocabulary and concept learning.

In traditional RT models, a designated student reads an assigned text aloud once before beginning discussion in groups. However, research by Millis et al. (1998) noted that during a second (oral) reading, readers were able to allocate increased attention to vocabulary and text comprehension. Because EAL students in particular tend to focus on the pronunciation rather than the meaning of unknown words in oral reading activities, Carla decided to have her students read the text silently before reading orally. This extra step was especially helpful for her EAL learners, who were often unsure of the correct pronunciation of new words and referred to their electronic 'talking dictionaries' to hear pronunciation models. Carla's addition of the initial silent reading stage to the RT process was intended to provide her students with increased opportunities to learn the meanings, sounds and spellings of new words as well as to increase their reading comprehension.

Carla explicitly taught the discourse structures that her students needed to ask for and give definitions. Her students prepared and used 'cue card' bookmarks with sample sentence frames serving as examples of the language forms they needed to perform each of the communicative functions of the major RT strategy roles (predicting, clarifying, questioning and summarizing) and of other strategies used in the RT group discussions, such as defining, justifying and paraphrasing.

Learning to use reading strategies

Before beginning small group work, Carla worked hard to prepare her students to use each of the four RT strategies. The first RT reading strategy introduced to the class was *prediction*. Carla read sections of text aloud and modelled how to make predictions, thinking aloud and explaining how she developed each hypothesis. She encouraged students to make personal connections with the text, relating it to other experiences. 'I wonder what this is about?' she would muse, looking through the book. 'I think it's going to be about … Oh, now I see …' Questioning the text before reading in this way encouraged all of her students to access prior knowledge and try to make connections with what they already knew. For her EAL learners, hearing other students verbalize their assumptions and expectations helped fill in some of the experiential gaps and translate previously implicit understandings into explicit statements. Students discussed the meaning of inference and gave examples and non-examples of logical inferences.

Carla encouraged her students to use information in the text to actively construct and predict meaning while reading. During reading, she directed their attention to the text structure as a resource for predicting. They were reminded to look at the headings, pictures, tables and graphs in their science textbooks. Carla constantly modelled and talked through her own predictions: 'I wonder what will be next … Oh, I think this next section will be about spiders having babies . . . Yes, I see the picture shows a spider with babies on its back and the last sentence said that they raise their young in many ways.'

She recorded her students' predictions on the board, including the reasoning behind their predictions (for instance a chapter title or prior information), and predictions were revised based on new information in the text. Her voice conveyed her enthusiasm: 'Wow, the author really tricked me there!' Or, 'Yes, I was right!' Students joined in this process and were asked to record and report their own predictions and explain the logical basis. Some of the EAL students initially copied and repeated Carla's models verbatim, but they were encouraged to add their own contributions when they were able to express their ideas. Requiring all of her students to justify their predictions helped them to make logical connections explicit. For her EAL students, however, this requirement provided a valuable opportunity to extend and elaborate on verbal responses that might otherwise have been limited to single words and short phrases (Verplaetse, 2007).

Once most students were comfortable using prediction as a strategy before and during reading, Carla decided that it was time to explicitly teach the next RT reading strategy: *clarification*. In RT, clarifying refers to requesting or providing meaning at the word, phrase or sentence level. The skills associated with the strategy of clarifying in Carla's class focused on what students could do to solve vocabulary and comprehension problems as they read. Carla first demonstrated to the class different ways of figuring out unknown words and how to decipher meaning embedded in the words and symbols in the text. Each RT period included some time during which word identification and decoding were addressed. Again, Carla used the 'think aloud' technique to model these skills: 'I don't know what this word is. I'll look at the first sounds. Are there any little words in it? Oh, I see the word ... I think the word is ...'

She also verbalized the possible thinking involved in using context to derive meanings for unknown words: 'I don't understand this word ... Maybe I should go back and read the sentence looking for clues. Oh, now I think I know. It must mean ... I see a comma there and the word that means almost the same is right after it. Yes, now I know.' Or: 'I don't know what that means. Maybe I should go back and read the sentence before it. I'm still not sure so I'll read ahead. Yes, now I understand. The next sentence explains the word.'

Once students were working independently in their RT groups, Carla observed that her students typically spent half of the RT group time clarifying the meaning of new words and concepts. The other half was divided among the other three main RT strategies: predicting, questioning, summarizing. She noted that her students became more comfortable using the language of definition as well as the language of clarification and summary, all important academic language functions in school.

Adapting and implementing RT in Miki's class

The second RT class example is set within an adult EAL programme administered through a large school district. Like Carla, Miki is an experienced teacher with a graduate diploma in EAL. In her EAL class of 17 students (aged 18 to 53), most have been in the USA for less than one year and have come from different countries in Latin America, Asia and the Caribbean. More than half of these students had completed a secondary diploma before leaving their home countries and hope to continue their education in the USA; several others have accompanied a spouse with similar goals. Most of these EAL students have a low intermediate level of English ability, and all have enrolled in Miki's class to improve their oral English communication skills.

Because of her students' diverse personal and professional interests, and because the adult EAL programme did/does not require a set curriculum or standardized assessments, Miki was able to select materials and topics covering a range of issues. Her curriculum content goals included helping her EAL students develop historical and contemporary knowledge of US culture and providing them with opportunities to explore different perspectives on important social issues (such as immigration, racial identity, and gender roles). Each week she chose (or asked students to select) two articles from a class set of newspapers published for adolescent and adult EAL newcomers to the USA. The articles in this serial covered current events of high interest value written at a low level (3rd or 4th grade) of reading difficulty.

The advanced educational level of many of Miki's students was a good indicator that they had strong literacy skills in their native language, and several were also able to read with comprehension in English. However, Miki believed that all of her students could benefit from RT if it were adapted to their language learning needs, and she targeted two specific processes in her adaptation and implementation of RT for this class: *peer interaction* and a *focus on the language forms* her students needed to participate in small group discussions of text. Both processes have been identified as factors contributing to second language acquisition, and Miki believed that they could be incorporated productively into the RT process. Through structured small group interaction and negotiation of meaning around texts as well as a collaborative focus on language form, she hoped that her students' regular participation in RT would improve their ability to communicate effectively in spoken English and to read with fluency as well as comprehension.

Interaction and second language learning

Research in second language acquisition strongly suggests that collaborative interaction (including interaction between EAL speakers) can assist EAL development through conversational scaffolding (for example Donato, 1994; Ohta, 1995). However, in classroom practice, many cooperative learning tasks fail to require participation by all group members or fail to assign specific roles for individual students. Adult EAL students are often unaccustomed to group work in the (language) classroom and may resist participating in unstructured group discussions with other EAL learners. The original RT model did not require participation by all group members, so Miki decided to rotate the four RT strategy roles with each new section of text (each section consisting of between one and three paragraphs, depending on paragraph length). Rotating the RT roles more frequently ensured that all students had greater opportunities and specific purposes for participating during each RT class session. Miki also expanded the focus of these roles to include oral reading fluency and accuracy, question formation, pronunciation, definition, and summarization.

Focus on language form

Second language acquisition research has also found that drawing adolescent and adult EAL learners' attention to selected language forms and functions can facilitate their learning of these forms (Doughty and Williams, 1998; Lightbown and Spada, 1990; Long, 1996; Lyster and Ranta, 1997). Miki defined a focus on form in the RT groups as explicit attention to the pronunciation of words, the grammatical structure of questions, and the discourse structure of definitions and summaries. As her students identified and defined new words, asked and answered questions about the text, and summarized main ideas, they were encouraged to notice the phonological, morphological, grammatical and discourse forms used for these functions.

As with Carla's class, Miki's students prepared and used 'cue card' bookmarks with sample sentence frames that served as scaffolds for their own language use and for corrective peer feedback. Sample sentence frames for providing feedback on meaning or pronunciation included: 'Excuse me, but I think that word is pronounced ___ (or means ___).' And, 'Are you sure that's right? Could it be ___?' Sample sentence frames for summarization included: 'This section is about (noun/phrase).' And, 'The main point of this reading is (that + clause).' Miki's students used these sentence frames to support their participation in the RT roles and to focus on the language forms needed to do so.

Although some adult EAL students are reluctant to speak out for fear of making mistakes, many students welcome feedback on their pronunciation (Parrino, 1998) and on other aspects of English language use. However, fluent English speakers often hesitate to question or correct EAL speakers unless their meaning is unclear. Therefore, EAL learners at intermediate and higher levels of English proficiency typically receive insufficient feedback on their errors and have limited opportunities for English language development. Drawing on her own belief that explicit feedback helps learners 'notice the gap' between their own and target language forms (Doughty, 2001; Long, 2003), Miki encouraged and prepared her students to provide feedback to their peers on their accuracy in English while engaging in text-based discussion in their RT groups.

Reading strategy roles

Miki adapted the RT process and reading strategy roles for her EAL class in a number of ways. Like Carla, Miki did not want her EAL students to have to read unfamiliar texts aloud in the RT groups. Miki first introduced each of the RT texts by leading a brief discussion based on the *predicting* strategy with the whole class. She then asked students to read the designated text independently prior to the RT group discussions. Pre-reading predictions were revisited as a whole group following each RT class session.

In the RT class sessions, the *Reader*'s role was to focus group members' attention on pronunciation, stress and intonation patterns of words, phrases and sentences, and on oral fluency. To begin an adapted RT session, the Reader read a predetermined section of text aloud and often requested help with pronunciation. Following the oral reading, other group members were allowed to correct the Reader. If the correct pronunciation of a word could not be determined during the RT group discussion, students consulted a dictionary and highlighted these words for the entire class to review with the teacher at the end of class. The follow-up class review allowed Miki to provide an oral reading model for the now-familiar text. She also used this time to teach five-minute 'mini-lessons' that focused specifically on troublesome phonological or ortho-graphic patterns in the highlighted vocabulary.

The second role in the RT group process was that of *Word Watcher*. This role addressed the important goal of vocabulary development, an ongoing need for EAL learners at all English proficiency levels. Although many new words are learned through multiple exposures in everyday social settings outside school, technical terms and their associated patterns of use in academic content areas are much less common and require more focused attention. The more oppor-tunities EAL learners have to hear, see and use a new word in a meaningful context, the more likely they are to remember it and incorporate it into their productive vocabulary. By discussing new words in the context of reading, students are able to process word meanings and forms at greater depth than by referring to a dictionary definition.

Following the oral reading of the text, the Word Watcher identified target vocabulary (including idiomatic expressions) for group discussion. Other group members were free to nominate words or phrases, and all students were expected to attempt to determine the meaning of unknown words using the context of the reading. When this was not possible, students were encouraged to define an unknown word by breaking it into smaller units and analysing its structure (its root, its suffix) and its grammatical role or function (as subject, or descriptor). Dictionaries were consulted only as a last resort.

The *Questioner* role followed the Word Watcher as the third strategy role in Miki's adapted RT process. Questioning served two distinct purposes: to clarify comprehension of the text, and to provide practice using the linguistic form and function of questions in English. The RT process provided group members with opportunities to clarify their understanding of the text (using questions of Who, What, When, How and Why) as well as providing opportunities for practice and feedback on their use of different question forms. Because questioning is such an important communicative function in both social interaction and academic discourse, and because many EAL students find the grammatical construction of questions difficult, Miki hoped that this RT role would help her students gain greater control over questioning in English. The corrective feedback provided within the RT groups on the accuracy of question forms was also potentially valuable as EAL students rarely receive this type of information in conversations outside the classroom.

Because Miki observed that there were some students for whom uptake did not occur even though their classmates explicitly corrected them, she incorpo-rated a written component into the RT process. She limited Questioners to two questions and had students write them on index cards along with the writer's name. Group members were then to proofread the questions and discuss any inaccuracies discovered. Miki found that adding this element forced those students who focused on oral communication to the exclusion of form to attend to their errors. She also noticed students repeating the questions once they had arrived at the final revision. At the end of the RT sessions, Miki would collect the cards and analyse the errors the students produced, as well as the corrections the group made, and she then used that information to guide instruction, both for the class as a whole and for individual students.

Finally, the role of the *Summarizer* was to synthesize information and paraphrase main ideas in the text. Beyond providing a final check on comprehension of the passage, the Summarizer role provided opportunities to practise synthesizing ideas in text and creating summary statements with key words from the text. It also provided models for the academic discourse functions of reporting, synthesizing and supporting main ideas. Miki's students' RT bookmarks included sample sentence frames such as: 'The author argues that ...' Students found the Summarizer to be the most challenging of the RT strategy roles, both cognitively and linguistically. One student commented during class, 'The Summarizer role is like broccoli. You don't like it, but it's good for you.'

See Appendix 6.1 for a table summarizing adaptations made by Carla and Miki to the original RT model.

Analysing the integration of language and content in the two RT classes

Both Miki and Carla used the RT structure to integrate language and content instruction in their classes with EAL learners. In both classes, student interaction and strategy instruction and use remained central components of the RT learning process, and both teachers targeted vocabulary and oral language development for their students. Both teachers emphasized the form/function connection and explicitly taught the language forms their students needed to participate in the RT group discussions. In many ways, these teachers' classes share essential characteristics. There are some important differences, however, in the extent to which they integrate language and content instruction and address language development goals for their EAL students. Applying the four questions introduced earlier to these teachers' adaptations of RT, we turn first to Carla's 3rd grade science class to see how she has addressed the first pair of questions.

Carla's RT Class

> 1a. Do the concepts in the curriculum or the texts or tasks in your instruction assume background knowledge or require skills that some EAL students may lack and that can prevent them from learning?

The state standards for the 3rd grade science curriculum require that students understand the principle of scientific inquiry. Carla knew that forming hypotheses, designing an experiment, and collecting data to answer an authentic question would be unfamiliar concepts for some of her EAL students. She could not assume that they were familiar with the practice of classifying objects according to their physical attributes rather than their purpose or function. Nor could she assume that they would be able to name or even recognize the most common local flora and fauna. Carla understood the linguistic dimension of these new experiences and knew that all of her students needed to learn the technical language associated with the science content. Her EAL students, however, faced the additional challenge of learning the genre-related, procedural language such as 'predict', 'measure' and 'confirm', as well as the more general vocabulary that her native English-speaking students already controlled, such as 'bark', 'roots', and the semantic distinctions between 'shrub' and 'bush'. Carla addressed the gaps in her EAL students' linguistic and conceptual knowledge by answering the second part of this question.

1b. If so, how can the linguistic, cultural and conceptual demands of the curriculum and your instruction be mediated so that all students have an opportunity to learn?

Carla understood the difficulty her EAL students faced in reading to learn from the science textbook. Although she did not simplify the language of the text, she modified the RT process to address her EAL students' linguistic and cultural differences and make the science content more understandable. Carla addressed the differences in her students' prior knowledge by providing relevant foundational experiences before reading. She incorporated demonstrations, field experiences, and hands-on activities to bridge the conceptual and linguistic gap for her EAL students. Carla's use (and her students' use) of the think-aloud technique also served to mediate the language and content learning demands in her classroom.

Carla formed RT groups primarily on the basis of students' reading levels and personalities. When possible she composed RT groups of EAL students and supportive English-proficient speakers, and she allowed groups with EAL members to skip non-essential sections of the text in order to reduce the volume of reading and the time needed to complete them. EAL students with very low English proficiency were paired with other EAL students from the same language background but with stronger English language skills. For example, one of Carla's students began the school year with virtually no ability to read, write or speak in English. Carla initially paired him with an RT partner who shared his native language and helped him to understand the reading by talking about the text in their common language, and to perform his RT roles by speaking for the pair in English.

Cue cards with model sentence frames provided students with the language support they needed to perform their RT strategy roles and participate effectively in the RT group discussions. (Note that this is a different purpose from using these sentence frames as instructional material to teach the language forms associated with the RT roles and through which the reading strategy functions are performed.)

Carla was indeed aware of and attentive to the linguistic and conceptual demands of the science curriculum of the language and culture learning needs of her EAL students. She used the structure and process of RT as a means of integrating language and content learning for all of her students. Although she deliberately highlighted the discourse and carefully modelled the language her students needed to participate in the RT groups, Carla's primary instructional foci were the content of the science curriculum and her students' ability to use the RT reading strategies. Language was recognized as an important and necessary tool for learning; however, instructional objectives for her students' language learning were determined by the conceptual content of the science curriculum and the cognitive/reading strategies of the RT process.

Thus, Carla's classroom reflects an integrated approach to language and content teaching that is weighted more heavily on content than on language. However, her own understanding of the role of language in learning is deeper than that of many teachers, and her attention to her EAL students' needs for academic language support and development is broader in scope and sharper in focus than that of most teachers of language-sensitive (sheltered) content classes. We can invoke the image of a continuum in considering a more appropriate designation/description for Carla's RT science class instruction, such as *'language rich'* or (*enhanced*) content instruction.

Miki's RT class

We next examine how Miki addressed the first set of questions in her adult EAL classroom. Like Carla, Miki understood the linguistic and cultural needs of her EAL students and acknowledged these in her modifications to RT. Also like Carla, she attempted to mediate the differences in her students' English language and literacy skills by pairing students with very low English proficiency with those who had stronger English skills and who could (and would) be supportive of their peers. Unlike Carla, however, Miki avoided pairing students from the same language background, and she encouraged students to use English in their RT group discussions whenever possible. Unlike Carla, Miki purposefully lowered the language demands of the RT texts and tasks by choosing materials written at a lower reading level than most of her students needed. Using texts that were relatively easy to read allowed more of her students to read with comprehension and participate more fully in the RT discussions. It also allowed her to structure the RT tasks around oral language development goals for her students. Unlike Carla, Miki's instructional emphasis in her RT class was clearly on the second set of questions.

> 2a. What aspects of linguistic and sociocultural competence are necessary for my EAL students to participate fully and equitably in school and society?

Miki and her adult students knew that their ability to communicate fluently, accurately and appropriately in English would improve their chances of success in academic, professional and social settings. As post-secondary students in the USA, they would need to define terms for abstract concepts, read critically, and participate in fast-paced group discussions, questioning, supporting and summarizing ideas. They wanted to be able to perform these academic language skills with fluency and accuracy in English. In professional and social settings they would need to be able to speak fluently and appropriately on diverse topics. They had to be informed about current events, recognize and understand popular references, and negotiate a wide range of interpersonal communication demands (Duff, 2001), most of which seemed quite daunting for Miki's students. In order to help her students reach these English language communication goals, Miki focused her attention on addressing the next question.

2b. How can I help them develop these aspects of academic, social and cultural competence in my classroom?

We can see that Miki's modifications to the RT process not only served to mediate the difficulty of the RT texts and tasks for her students; they also reflected her explicit attention to developing their English language proficiency. Her requirement for students to read assigned texts prior to the RT class sessions allowed them to read initially for meaning and gave them time to focus on the sound/symbol connections between oral and written English and on the patterns of word forms and sentence structures for selected language functions, such as questions, definitions and summaries. Miki used RT as a structure for collaborative interaction and a focus on language form to advance her students' English development. She modified the process of rotating RT roles, requiring each group member to participate in and to assume several different roles in each RT class session. This modification expanded the opportunities for each student to use the RT strategies and practise the target language structures. Structuring peer feedback for her students on their accuracy reflected Miki's understanding of the language learning potential of 'noticing' the forms of language and of the importance of feedback on errors.

Summary

In sum, we see that with respect to the four curriculum planning questions, the first set of questions emphasizes EAL learners' access to the content curriculum. While both teachers address content learning and issues of comprehensibility for their EAL students, Carla's RT instruction reflects a stronger focus on academic content learning. The second set of questions addresses EAL students' development of linguistic and cultural competence in school settings. Again, while both teachers attend to their EAL students' language development, Miki's RT class weights language learning objectives more heavily than does Carla's. This comparison of these two classes does not represent an assessment of instructional effectiveness or an evaluation of teacher quality. The relative emphasis of language and content for each group seems perfectly appropriate given these learners and the learning contexts.

Applying the construct of a continuum of emphasis on language or content to compare the differences in these two teachers' approaches to integrating language and content instruction, we see that Miki's adaptations to RT reflect a strong, explicit emphasis on English language development. Her students' need to improve their spoken English motivated her decision to shift the traditional focus of RT from reading comprehension through strategy instruction to emphasize *oral* language learning through strategy-based discussions of texts.

Miki's RT class is positioned more towards the language development end of the continuum, and her class represents a clear example of content-based language instruction.

Carla's RT class reflects the more dominant role of the academic curriculum in K-12 school contexts. Her RT class provided students with instruction and practice in the use of reading strategies to improve their reading comprehension and content learning. Her adaptations to RT provided her EAL students with opportunities for interaction in collaborative group discussions, scaffolded support in academic language use, and vocabulary development that could help all of her students in learning to read and reading to learn in English. Carla's class is therefore situated more towards the end of the continuum emphasizing content learning. It represents an exceptionally strong example of language-sensitive content learning.

In reality, all students in both teachers' classes needed to develop their vocabulary and reading comprehension in English. And all of the EAL students in both classes also needed ongoing instruction and support in their oral language development in English, including development in the cultural background knowledge and social/pragmatic skills necessary to express themselves fully and appropriately. One could argue that the age of Miki's (adult) students made it easier for them to focus on the forms and functions of English and to take the metalinguistic perspective needed to reflect on their own strategy use and language learning. Also, the fact that Miki had EAL students (only) in her class gave her a clarity of focus and level of freedom that Carla did not have in integrating language and content for her class of EAL and English-proficient students. Other variables among students and within learning contexts can influence a teacher's ability to fully attend to (both) EAL students' language and content learning needs. We turn next to a brief discussion of some of these considerations and constraints.

Considerations

The current standardization of K-12 learning expectations for all (including EAL) students means that teachers have very little discretion in changing the scope and sequence of the curriculum and their instruction. In addition, the placement of EAL students in mainstream classes without specialized EAL classes to support their English language development makes it extremely difficult for them to receive either the sheltered content instruction or the focused, content-based language and culture support that many need to succeed in school. In fact, we doubt that any individual teacher can provide sufficient support, and we believe that the old adage, 'It takes a whole village to raise a child', applies particularly well to EAL learners: 'It takes a whole school to educate a student.' This implies that all teachers (not just EAL specialists) must understand how language and culture influence learning in school. Content area teachers must be willing and able to support students' second language and literacy development as well as their academic content area learning. It also means that EAL specialist teachers must ground their instructional goals in the linguistic and cultural knowledge and skills required by the school context and curriculum. Certainly, EAL teachers cannot assume the disciplinary expertise and instructional roles of other content teachers. Similarly, the expertise and roles of EAL teachers cannot be subsumed by teachers of English language arts, reading, or other subjects. Rather, EAL teachers and other content area teachers must coordinate their distinct, complementary roles to provide a coherent curriculum and comprehensible instruction.

Assuming responsibility for new dimensions of curriculum and instruction can be challenging and even intimidating for both language teachers and content area teachers. Other complicating issues have been identified, including epistemological and status differences between EAL and other subject area teachers (Arkoudis, 2006; Creese, 2002; 2006; Franson, 1999). When EAL and content teachers collaborate, the language curriculum typically takes a subordinate role to content-learning objectives, and EAL teachers are positioned as language teaching 'assistants' to their subject area colleagues.

Davison and Williams (2001) have noted that an equal balance of attention to language and content learning is difficult to achieve. However, we are not convinced that an equal balance is essential, as the emphasis on language or content will necessarily shift in response to teacher, learner and contextual variables. In addition, attention to language development can be achieved collaboratively across faculty assignments as well as encouraged within individual teachers. Unfortunately, instructional collaborations between EAL and other content teachers seem to be 'exceptional' rather than the norm, particularly at the secondary level. Also lacking are the institutional support structures needed for successful team teaching, such as administrative support, planning time, and 'ongoing, research oriented professional development' (TESOL, 2008). A better understanding of, and stronger teacher preparation and systematic support for collaborative, complementary teaching will be essential to the effective integration of language, culture and content instruction for EAL learners.

Future possibilities

The complex, long-term nature of academic language learning requires that faculties share responsibility for providing EAL students with access to appropriate content teaching and 'focused language instruction' based on the academic curriculum and targeted to their language and culture learning needs (Goldenberg, 2008). Reciprocal teaching is just one of a number of structured techniques that can serve multiple language and content teaching goals (such as oral language, vocabulary, reading, strategy use, and content). Although the traditional RT model may be considered an effective technique with some EAL learners, Carla and Miki found it necessary to modify RT for their EAL students. Examining what makes Carla's and Miki's classrooms effective learning environments for EAL students can help us understand the nature of appropriate curriculum development and teaching and assessment practices in integrated language and content instruction.

Points for reflection

1   What individual learner characteristics (for example, age/grade, English proficiency, motivation for learning English) may have influenced these teachers' integration of language and content instruction for these students?
2   What contextual variables (for example, required curriculum objectives, number of EAL students in a class, linguistic and cultural homogeneity of students) may have influenced these two teachers' approaches to integrating language and content instruction in their classes?
3   How might other factors affect or limit a teacher's ability to integrate language and content instruction? (Sample factors include student attitudes or willingness to focus on language in content classes, content teachers' lack of language expertise, language teachers' lack of content expertise, lack of opportunities for professional development, and lack of collaboration with other teachers.)
4   Given the specified learner and contextual variables, in what ways might Carla and/or Miki strengthen their attention to language, culture, and content learning for their students?

Suggestions for further reading

Goldenberg, C. (2008) 'Teaching English language learners: What the research does – and does not – say', *American Educator* (Summer): 8–44.

Jameson, J. (1998) 'Teaching the text backwards', *Theory into Practice 7*. www.cal.org/cc14/ttp7.htm.

TESOL (2006) *Pre K-12 English Language Proficiency Standards*. Alexandria, VA: TESOL.

TESOL (2008) *Position Statement on Teacher Preparation for Content-Based Instruction (CBI)*. www.tesol.org/s_tesol/seccss.asp?CID=32&DID=37.

Verplaetse, L. S. (2007) 'Developing academic language through an abundance of interaction', in L. S. Verplatse and N. Migliacci (eds), *Inclusive Pedagogy for English Language Learners: A Handbook of Research-informed Practices*. Mahwah, NJ: Lawrence Erlbaum Associates (pp. 167–180).

Notes

1   Academic language includes all of the aspects of language needed to 'access and engage with the school curriculum' (Bailey and Heritage, 2008).
2   Both teachers were engaged in classroom-based research on implementing RT in their classrooms.

References

Arkoudis, S. (2006) 'Negotiating the rough ground between ESL and mainstream teachers', *International Journal of Bilingual Education and Bilingualism*, 9 (4): 415–33.

Bailey, A. and Heritage, M. (2008) *Formative Assessment for Literacy, Grades K-6: Building Reading and Academic Language Skills Across the Curriculum*. Newbury Park, CA: Corwin Press.

Cantoni-Harvey, G. (1987) *Content-area Language Instruction: Approaches and Strategies*. Reading, MA: Addison-Wesley.

Chamot, A. U. and O'Malley, J. M. (1994) *The CALLA Handbook: Implementing the Cognitive Academic Language Learning Approach*. Reading, MA: Addison-Wesley.

Crandall, J. A. (ed.) (1995) *ESL Through Content-area Instruction*. Washington, DC: Center for Applied Linguistics.

Creese, A. (2002) 'Discursive construction of power in teacher relationships', *TESOL Quarterly*, 36 (4): 597–616.

Creese, A. (2006) 'Supporting talk? Partnership teachers in classroom interaction', *International Journal of Bilingual Education and Bilingualism*, 9 (4): 434–53.

Davison, C. and Williams, A. (2001) '*Integrating language and content: Unresolved issues*', in B. Mohan, C. Leung and C. Davison (eds), *English as a Second Language in the Mainstream: Teaching, Learning and Identity*. Harlow: Pearson.

Donato, R. (1994) 'Collective scaffolding in second language learning', in J. P. Lantolf and G. Appel (eds), *Vygotskian Approaches to Second Language Research*. Norwood, NJ: Ablex (pp. 33–56).

Doughty, C. (2001) 'Cognitive underpinnings of focus on form', in P. Robinson (ed.), *Cognition and Second Language Instruction*. Cambridge: Cambridge University Press (pp. 206–57).

Doughty, C. and Williams, J. (eds) (1998) *Focus on Form in Classroom Second Language Acquisition*. Cambridge: Cambridge University Press.

Duff, P. A. (2001) 'Language, literacy, content, and (pop) culture: Challenges for ESL students in mainstream courses', *The Canadian Modern Language Review*, 58 (1): 103–32.

Echevarria, J., Vogt, M. and Short, D. (2004) *Making Content Comprehensible for English Language Learners: The SIOP model*, 2nd edn. Needham Heights, MA: Allyn & Bacon.

Faltis, C. (1993) 'Critical issues in the use of sheltered content teaching in high school bilingual programs', *Peabody Journal of Education*, 69 (1): 136–51.

Franson, C. (1999) 'Mainstreaming learners of English as an additional language: the class teacher's perspective', *Language, Culture, and Curriculum*, 12 (1): 59–70.

Freeman, D. E. and Freeman, Y. S. (2000) *Teaching Reading in Multilingual Classrooms*. Portsmouth, NH: Heinemann.

Goldenberg, C. (2008) 'Teaching English language learners: What the research does – and does not – say', *American Educator* (Summer): 8–44.

Harper, C. A. and de Jong, E. J. (2005) 'Working with ELLs: What's the difference?', in A. Huerta Macias (ed.), *Working with English Language Learners: Perspectives and Practice*. Dubuque, IA: Kendall Hunt (pp. 107–35).

Jameson, J. (1998) 'Teaching the text backwards', *Theory into Practice 7*. www.cal.org/cc14/ttp7.htm.

Kaufman, D. and Crandall, J. A. (eds) (2005) *TESOL Case Studies in TESOL Practice: Content-based ESL*. Alexandria, VA: TESOL.

Lightbown, P. and Spada, N. (1990) 'Focus on form and corrective feedback in communicative language teaching', *Studies in Second Language Acquisition*, 12: 429–48.

Long, M. (1996) 'The role of the linguistic environment in second language acquisition', in W. Ritchie and T. K. Bhatia (eds), *Handbook of Second Language Acquisition*. San Diego, CA: Academic Press (pp. 413–68).

Long, M. (2003) *Task-based Language Teaching*. Oxford: Blackwell.

Lyster, R. and Ranta, L. (1997) 'Corrective feedback and learners' uptake: Negotiation of form in communicative classrooms', *Studies in Second Language Acquisition*, 19: 37–66.

Marks, M., Pressley, M., Coley, J. D., Craig, S., Gardner, R., DePinto, T. and Rose, W. (1993) 'Three teachers' adaptations of reciprocal teaching in comparison to traditional reciprocal teaching', *Elementary School Journal*, 94: 267–83.

Millis, K. K., Simon, S. and tenBroek, N. S. (1998) 'Resource allocation during the rereading of scientific texts', *Memory and Cognition*, 26: 232–46.

Ohta, A. (1995) 'Applying sociocultural theory to an analysis of learner discourse: Learner–learner collaborative interaction in the zone of proximal development', *Issues in Applied Linguistics*, 6: 93–122.

Olsen, L. (1997) *Made in America: Immigrant Students in our Public Schools*. New York: New Press.

Palincsar, A. S. and Brown, A. L. (1984) 'Reciprocal teaching of comprehension-fostering and comprehension-monitoring activities', *Cognition and Instruction*, 1: 117–75.

Parrino, A. (1998) 'The politics of pronunciation and the adult learner', in T. Smoke (ed.), *Adult ESL: Politics, Pedagogy, and Participation in Classroom and Community Program*. Mahwah, NJ: Lawrence Erlbaum Associates (pp. 171–84).

Pica, T. (1994) 'Research on negotiation: What does it reveal about second-language learning conditions, processes, and outcomes?', *Language Learning*, 44: 493–527.

Rosenshine, B. and Meister, C. (1994) 'Reciprocal teaching: A review of the research', *Review of Educational Research*, 64: 479–530.

Stoller, F. L. (2004) 'Content-based instruction: Perspectives on curriculum planning', *Annual Review of Applied Linguistics*, 24: 261–83.

Swain, M. and Lapkin, S. (1998) 'Interaction and second language learning: Two adolescent French immersion students working together', *Modern Language Journal*, 82: 320–37.

TESOL (2008) *Position Statement on Teacher Preparation for Content-Based Instruction (CBI)*. www.tesol.org/s_tesol/seccss.asp?CID=32&DID=37.

Verplaetse, L. S. (2007) 'Developing academic language through an abundance of interaction', in L. S. Verplatse and N. Migliacci (eds), *Inclusive Pedagogy for English Language Learners: A Handbook of Research-informed Practices*. Mahwah, NY: Lawrence Erlbaum Associates (pp. 167–180).

Appendix 6.1   Differences in Palincsar and Brown's RT model (1984) and the RT models adapted by Carla and Miki

Original RT model	Carla's RT adaptations	Miki's RT adaptations
Population: Native English speakers (middle grades)	Population: Native English speakers *and EAL students* (middle grades)	Population: *EAL students only* (adolescent/adult)
Purpose: Assist reading comprehension through reading strategy instruction and discussion of text	Purpose: Assist reading comprehension, *content learning, and vocabulary and English language development* through reading strategy instruction, *collaborative interaction,* and discussion of content area textbook	Purpose: Assist reading comprehension, *oral language development (reading fluency and pronunciation, and grammatical accuracy* through reading strategy instruction, collaborative interaction, and discussion *of social/cultural issues*
Practice: Groups of 4–7	Practice: Groups of *4–5*; EAL students from same native language paired to *allow translation as needed to assist with comprehension of content area concepts*	Practice: Groups of *3–4*; EAL students from same native language separated to *avoid translation and require negotiation of meaning in English*
Preparation: 10 class sessions of initial strategy instruction by the teacher and strategy practice by students before independent use in small RT groups	Preparation: *12* class sessions of initial **strategy** Instruction and *6 sessions of modelling the RT process* by the teacher, then *3 sessions of guided small group work* using 1–2 strategies	Preparation: 2 class sessions of explanation and practice of the strategy roles and RT process
Process: A single leader controls all strategies used in the small group discussion of a text. The discussion leader role shifts as the group moves on to the next text selection or the next RT class session	Process: Each small group member controls a *single strategy* in the small group discussion of each section of text. Use of each strategy is elicited from all group members in each RT class session. *Strategy roles shift in each RT class session*	Process: Each small group member uses a *single strategy* in small group discussion for each section of text. *Strategy roles shift each time the group moves on to the next section of text* (within the same RT class session)

(Continued)

Appendix 6.1   *(Continued)*

Original RT model	Carla's RT adaptations	Miki's RT adaptations
Process: Initial oral reading, then discussion in small groups	Process: *Initial introduction of the reading topic by a pre-reading activity and group discussion* led by the teacher. Initial *silent reading then oral reading and discussion in small groups*	Process: *Initial introduction of a new topic and group discussion led by the teacher. Independent reading of assigned text completed before each RT class session*
Process: Strategy roles are performed in the following order (by the group leader): 1 predicting (conducted in small groups before reading) 2 questioning 3 summarizing 4 clarifying	Process: Strategy roles are performed in this order (each strategy role is assumed by a different group member): 1 predicting (Predictor acts as the group leader, prompting other RT roles) 2 *clarifying* 3 *questioning* 4 *summarizing*	Process: Strategy roles are performed in this order: 1 *oral reading* (focus on fluency, pronunciation and intonation) 2 *word watching* (focus on vocabulary meaning and form) 3 questioning (focus on form and meaning) 4 summarizing (focus on meaning and form)

7

Sociocultural Approaches to Language Teaching and Learning

Margaret R. Hawkins

Introduction

English language teaching (ELT) is a relatively young field. In its earlier years, pedagogical models were taken from foreign language teaching, and based on views of language taken from structural linguistics. Thus to come to speak a language entailed learning its vocabulary, structures and forms, and practising these in scripted ways. Other chapters in this volume speak to changing views of language pedagogy, as the field has moved to communicative approaches, and those that teach language through content. A sociocultural approach does not displace these, and does not, in fact, proscribe particular texts or activities for language learning and teaching. Rather it entails a particular view of language, which I will explicate here, and a concomitant view of classrooms as spaces that can facilitate English language and literacy development that has implications for the structuring of the classroom environment and activities, and for the roles participants take within it.

A sociocultural view of language

A sociocultural approach, as its name implies, situates language use in its social and cultural contexts. Language, as a communicative tool, is always used by and between people for the purpose of making meaning. A language – English for our purposes here – is not one monolithic entity, but a variety of genres, registers, dialects and so forth that are used in specific spaces for specific purposes. While it is clear that different people use different forms of English, say African-American vernacular English (in the case of African Americans), or Singlish (in the case of Singaporeans), even that distinction is too uniform. Native-like fluency in a language requires that people have the ability to switch between different forms in different contexts for different purposes, fluently and effortlessly. Here is an example. Imagine that there has recently been a rash of gang-related violence in a neighbourhood very close to yours. You have a discussion about this with your best friend. Shortly afterwards, your grandmother phones. She is concerned because she has read about the gang violence, and wants to discuss it with you. If you take a minute to imagine those actual conversations, you will see that, although the general topic is the same, not only might the content of what you say be different, but the actual words and structures you use will likely be different too, as may intonation, pitch, and other aspects of language use. Differences may be attributed to generational differences, formality/informality, and so on, but are rooted in the relationships we have with those we are communicating with, what we are speaking about (imagine if you were instead speaking about the break-up of your latest relationship, or a professional accomplishment), the context in which the communication takes place, and what it is we wish to accomplish.

A sociocultural view of language posits that language use is about situated meaning-making, and meanings constructed in communication are not just based on language. Many other things convey meaning that go hand in hand with the language we use. Things such as gestures and facial expressions carry meaning. (Imagine someone saying, 'I especially liked the history lecture,' followed by a wink. The wink changes the meaning entirely.) But equally important are all of the other things that send messages about who people are (identities they are enacting) and wish to be seen as, such as their dress, or body language, or the tools and props that they use. These things work together with language, as people in real time in situated communications gauge who their interlocutors are, what their intentions are, and what they are trying to say even as they author their own words and actions, in the interplay of constructing meanings together. Being 'fluent' in a language means more than knowing vocabulary and structure; it means knowing which varieties of language to use, when, where, and to what purpose in local situated contexts.

Let us return to our imaginings. You are students, and your assignment is to do a presentation to the class on gang violence. Again, while the overall topic is the same, the language and structure you use might vary significantly from those in the two earlier discussions. But so might how you are dressed, where you are physically located and your stance (perhaps standing formally at the front of a classroom instead of curled up on the couch over a cup of tea), and the props you use (a PowerPoint presentation, a statistical chart, or a map). Additionally, what counts as knowledge and how you make knowledge claims differ, so opinions and anecdotal evidence won't do – you must draw from sources that are seen as academically legitimate and name them, and appear to present unbiased and depersonalized information. This is a crucial point. There are forms of language and ways of communicating that are specific to the culture of schooling, and that are rarely used outside of school or professional contexts. In order for English learners to succeed in school, they must master school-based forms of languages and literacies, and be able to show that they have mastered them by using them in the sorts of performances that count in school.

A sociocultural view of classrooms

Just as language use must be seen as a situated phenomenon, so must learning and teaching in classrooms. There are two key aspects to understanding how sociocultural theories might guide us to structure classrooms in ways that adequately support English learners.

Sociocultural theories draw on the work of Lev Vygotsky (1978), who posits that learning occurs through social interactions, as learners make meaning through the negotiation of new concepts (and language). His work, focused on children's learning, argues that learning occurs in a 'zone of proximal development' (ZPD), where children, through scaffolded interactions with more capable peers and adults, can move to the next stage of development (beyond their current stage). Learning, then, may be seen as a system of apprenticeship (Lave and Wenger, 1991; Rogoff, 1990). The requisite skills, knowledge and language for school success are distributed throughout the classroom environment, located in teachers, staff, students, texts, and other resources. Students come to understandings of school-based practices, concepts and language through scaffolded social negotiations and interactions with others, which are mediated by and through texts and materials. Understandings and knowledge are first external, as they are negotiated with others, then internalized as they are appropriated to become the child's own. This has clear implications for teachers. If learning occurs through social interaction, then classrooms must be explicitly organized to optimize opportunities for scaffolded social interactions through which learning may occur. This means minimizing (but not eradicating) the time teachers spend lecturing to students, and organizing tasks such that learners must work together *using language* to accomplish them. Careful attention must be paid to the sorts of scaffolding that English learners will need to participate successfully in such environments.

While this sociocultural view theorizes classrooms as spaces for learning, it is thus far limited to the world inside the classroom walls. The other important aspect of applications of sociocultural theories to classroom learning is that we cannot view what happens inside classrooms as distinct and separate from what happens outside of them. Classrooms are spaces where participants come together to engage in specific sorts of activities – those mandated by schools. Each participant (student, staff member, volunteer) comes with their own knowledge, experiences and backgrounds, rooted in their life histories and trajectories. Because meanings are made by relating new language and concepts to what we already know, and building on the foundations we bring, we (as teachers) must know what our students bring to school, so that we can leverage this to help them make sense of the activities, content and language of schooling. In this way we bridge the worlds of home and school. We can't assume that we (as teachers) know and understand the histories, experiences, ways of thinking, viewpoints and understandings of our students, nor that they share ours. And we know that curriculum, instructional approaches, and school environments may align with experiences that middle-class, mainstream, native English-speaking students bring to school, but not necessarily those of culturally and linguistically diverse students (see, for example, Heath, 1983; Tharp and Yamauchi, 1994; Valdes, 2001). This creates an unequal learning environment, set up to offer access to those who already come with knowledge and skills that align with those privileged in schools, but denying it to those who don't.

Commonly, teachers assume that their job is to assist students to assimilate to the practices of school. They feel that they must help students to adjust, and to engage with schooling, learning and living as mainstream students and families do. They operate from a deficit perspective; that is, these students come without the language, knowledge, resources and support that other children have, and teachers see their role as providing what the students need to catch up to others. Sociocultural theories, however, tell us that children do in fact come replete with knowledge, language skills, and rich family and community resources. They are simply different from what school people know to look for and recognize. Thus students receive the message that who they are and what they know does not count in this new environment.

In order for all students to learn, schools must value, validate and represent all languages and cultures of those in the school community. This is easy to do on a surface level, through typical multicultural events such as potlucks, acknowledging cultural holidays and celebrations, and displaying ethnic/cultural music, dances, costumes. However, while this is better than nothing, it fails to recognize, at a deeper level, what it means to be a member of a cultural and linguistic community. It fails to demand that teachers connect *as a learner* with the families and communities that their students come from, to learn about beliefs, world-views, and ways of being in and seeing the world that are different from their own, and then find ways to draw on and incorporate what they learn in their teaching (Gonzalez et al., 2005). It also fails to recognize the barriers that cultural and linguistic diversity create, both socially and academically. It fails to connect students to learning, it fails to connect students to each other as co-equals, and it fails to connect families with the academic practices of school. While newcomers certainly must learn the language and practices of schooling, educators also must change long-held beliefs and traditions regarding educational practices.

In order to demonstrate this, let me introduce two students who have recently immigrated. They are fictitious, although based on composite characteristics of real students. We will then identify some prototypical school events and activities, and think about how they affect these students and their families.

Chung-Ho is a male who came from Korea one year ago with his mother and younger sister. His father is a Samsung executive in Korea, and his mother was an elementary teacher when she lived there. His father is still in Korea working to support the family's dream of having their children attending school in an English-speaking country. His mother speaks some English, although not fluently, and is not currently working outside the home. They live in an area with a number of Korean families, and attend a Korean church.

Bashir and his family are refugees from Sudan. They fled from their village after the Janjaweed attacked, killing his father and capturing his younger brother. He has lived in a refugee camp in Chad for the past six years. He has not had any formal schooling. He arrived four months ago, and is currently living in government-sponsored housing. His mother has not yet begun to work; she is currently enrolled in English language classes. She has no formal schooling, and is not literate in her native language. He has three remaining brothers and four sisters, all of whom are under the age of 17.

While both of the students had arrived relatively recently, neither spoke English upon arrival, and both live in a household with only one parent present, there are significant differences in what they know and bring based on their life experiences. Let us imagine their engagement with the following aspects of schooling.

- *A literature project.* Students are asked to read a mystery novel, then create a diorama (in a shoe box) that represents a key event in the novel. They have two weeks to complete the project.

This is a project that students are expected to complete in out-of-school time. It requires not only the ability to read the novel, but knowledge of genres of literature. They must also have the supplies to build the diorama, and the understanding of how to do so appropriately. Chung-Ho will likely have the knowledge he needs to do this, albeit in Korean, given that he has received a good and consistent education prior to his arrival, and his mother was a teacher. If, however, he doesn't, he has an extended Korean community to turn to for help. Bashir, on the other hand, does not have these resources, having no prior formal education, no extended community, and no financial resources for purchasing art supplies. He has never read a mystery (or any) novel, as he is unable to read. And his mother does not have the resources to help him, in terms of academic support, finances, or time.

- *A science project.* Students are told that their school will be having a science fair. They have one month to prepare a project for display. Books are displayed to provide ideas, but the work is primarily to be done out of school. Prizes will be awarded; the winner goes to the state competition. Parents are expected to attend.

Some of the factors above apply here. The science fair is a prototypical school event; most of us have experienced them. It is likely that Chung-Ho has had this experience, but even if not he has help readily available. His mother was a teacher, he owns a computer and has research skills, knows what counts as 'science' and how to design and carry out projects. In addition, his father, as a Samsung engineer, will likely be able to provide ideas. He can afford to buy materials, and understands the competitive nature of these sorts of events. His mother is familiar with being expected to be involved in her child's schooling. As for Bashir, he has no model for an event of this sort. He doesn't know what a science fair is, and may not even know what 'science' or a scientist is, or what counts as being within the domain of science. He doesn't have the resources (knowledge, access to information, money, time and space) to do a project of this scope outside of school. And it is unlikely his parent will be able to attend. Even if she can understand the invitation (will it be in her language, and delivered orally?), she would not be comfortable in such an unfamiliar environment, won't speak the language to be able to participate, and may have trouble with transportation and childcare. (For a more indepth analysis of science fairs vis-à-vis culturally and linguistically responsive practices, see Hawkins and Nicoletti, 2008.)

- *A language arts project*. Students have just read a book, within the genre of adolescent literature, in which teenagers survive a shipwreck and are stranded on an island. Their assignment (to be done in class) is to pretend that they are one of the characters, and write a letter home to their parents.

This is an activity that calls for students to take on a fictitious identity, and imagine what someone else might think and feel. Not only is this a culturally bound concept, but it calls for familiarity with the context. Imagine your confusion if you had never seen an island, or a boat. While it is again likely that Chung-Ho will have encountered this sort of task in school, and have been encouraged to use his imagination in regard to reading (through questions such as, what would have happened if … ? Why do you think …?), Bashir would not have a history of the same sorts of interactions with texts (see Heath, 1982). Nor would he know the standard format or language of a letter, even if he had the English literacy skills to write one. It is unlikely, given his history, that he would have engaged much previously in what we think of as developmental play, and taken on other characters or spoken in a character role other than his own.

- *A social studies project*. Students are provided with a list of geographical terms, such as delta, isthmus, fjord, tributary, plain, gulf, and peninsula. They must find and write definitions for each, identify a real example, and draw a picture and label it.

Here students encounter language that is rarely (although sometimes) heard outside of school. And they are asked to do a school-based task: look up and copy definitions. Chung-Ho will likely have experience with reference materials, will know for instance how alphabetization works, and, as noted before, has a computer to assist his efforts. He will likely have familiarity with map skills, some prior exposure to notions of geographic characteristics, and know that different places have diverse geographical features. Again, he will have resources, human and material, available to him. He may understand the concepts in his first language, then have translation tools available to find the English words. Bashir, with no formal schooling, will not have encountered most of these terms, especially those features that are not represented in the region in which he has lived, which was largely desert. He won't have experience with reference materials, nor resources to help him.

These examples all represent typical school practices in their respective disciplinary areas. While more traditional approaches to language learning and teaching may see practices such as these as necessary to assimilating students to the language and practices of school, sociocultural approaches, while recognizing that students must have these skills in order to succeed in school, suggest that there may be more linguistically and culturally responsive ways to design and deliver instruction. We have seen, even in these few examples, that there are different forms of language demanded, which are not being explicitly taught. The words and structures used in writing a letter versus presenting a formal science project versus providing dictionary definitions vary significantly, although all are school-based (while the letter may be seen as more personal, there is still a formal structure required). Students unfamiliar with these genres, registers and forms are at a real disadvantage.

All of these activities have been designed for students to do by themselves, whether in or out of school. As discussed above, sociocultural approaches see learning as occurring in situated social interaction, and although in these examples students are expected to interact with texts, computers and materials – all of which mediate their understandings – they are not co-constructing and negotiating meanings together, and they are denied the scaffolding that comes from these interactions, as well as the practice in using school-based language.

Perhaps the most grievous loss here is the connection between school activities and what students know and bring. While in some cases, such as the diorama, modelling may help students to complete the project, none offers appropriate opportunities for students to draw on and build on their knowledge and experiences. For the science fair project, for example, either of these students may have had experiences that they could use to identify and design a project: Chung-Ho, perhaps, through technology, and Bashir, perhaps, through the natural world. Bashir will have experienced drought, and food shortage. Certainly they may have seen other sorts of geographical features for the social studies assignment, and could speak about those of their homes. And, for the language arts project, Bashir might have experiences he could tap into to discuss in his letter what it felt like to be uprooted, isolated, separated from all he has known. But teachers must recognize what students bring, and offer opportunities for making connections in sensitive and responsive ways.

An additional concern is the way in which these projects shut out families, as opposed to creating opportunities for connections. Assignments are given in class, with all communication between teacher and students. Communication with parents is limited. And when there are expectations of parents, it is in very prescribed ways: in these cases, the sole expectation is for parents to come to the science fair. In an instructional environment based on a sociocultural approach to schooling and learning that is truly linguistically and culturally responsive, communications will be delivered in ways that can be understood, accommodations will be made for participation, knowledge and skills of *all* parents will be drawn on and incorporated into activities, and parents will be connected to the curriculum and learning activities.

All of the examples offered above focus on classroom instructional activities. In addition to exploring curriculum and instructional practices, attention must be paid to the larger school environment, including extracurricular activities. All aspects of a school environment send messages to students about who they are and can be in school, and whether or not they belong here. For students, the ability to 'count' as a member of the school community, and take on the identity of a learner in school, contributes to academic success (Hawkins, 2005; Toohey, 2000). Let us explore the cultural and linguistic responsiveness of just a couple of examples of school-wide activities.

- *Open house.* An open house, or back-to-school-night, is a tradition in most schools. It is a time near the start of the school year for parents to enter their children's classrooms, meet their teachers, and receive information about what their children will be learning in the upcoming school year. There may also be information as to routines, transportation, and assessment measures, and forms to be filled out.

Both Chung-Ho's and Bashir's mother would benefit from having an interpreter available at such an occasion. Without one, only Chung-Ho's mother is likely to gain from the experience. She not only has some English, but is familiar with the routines of school, so already has a script to which she can attach new information. She also has an extended community to 'prep' her for the event, so she will know what information to look for and what questions to ask. Bashir's mother, in addition to childcare and transportation needs, will not understand explanations, even in her native language, as to subject matter and academic expectations. She will likely feel uncomfortable in an unfamiliar environment, and not know what to expect.

- *A school dance/prom.* Starting in late elementary or middle school, school-sponsored dances, including junior and senior prom, are viewed as not only a necessary social outlet, and beneficial to the social development of children, but even as a rite of passage.

School dances are, clearly, culturally laden activities, as forms of music and dance are culturally embedded, as are the routines surrounding these events. Our understandings of developmental appropriacy for adolescents is culturally bound, as are our views of gender roles in activities such as these. It is possible, for example, that Chung-Ho's family may think it inappropriate for pre-teens and teens to date.

Even if families are willing, there is much cultural knowledge entailed in successfully participating in prom. You must know how to arrange a date, buy a corsage/bouquet, perhaps hire a limo and make reservations for dinner, rent a tuxedo or buy an appropriate dress and so on. These are cultural scripts, as are the ways in which you are expected to engage with others (including the language you use, body language, and what you do) once you are at the actual event. While it's clear that lack of material resources may prohibit students from attending, so may lack of knowledge of the cultural scripts that are entailed. Chung-Ho may already have them, but if not he may have access to them in his extended community, and he has the material resources to enable him to go. Bashir has none of this.

   This points to the need for *all* students and families to have their voices included in decision-making about school events and activities. Schools must ensure that structures such as parent–teacher organizations represent all families, and that student organizations include all students.

Summing it up

As we have seen in the examples above, virtually all aspects of schooling entail cultural models of language use, learning and teaching, and activities designed to be developmentally appropriate that will not be equally familiar nor equally accessible to all students. This is not just because students are English learners, but because they come situated in particular histories, experiences, and lived realities, that carry with them ways of thinking, knowing, perceiving and acting. While students certainly must adjust to their new environment, and come to see themselves as active and equal participants in it, it is unreasonable to expect them to do so in an environment that is set up to create barriers for them, instead of offering appropriate support. It is the educators' responsibility to unpack the activities of classrooms and schools, and change current practices to be more inclusive of and responsive to diverse learners.

   In order to do this, educators should aim to do the following:

- Vary participation patterns for lessons such that students engage with others in activities that call for active communication and negotiation of meanings.
- Ensure that lessons and activities are designed to leverage the knowledge and experiences that students bring.
- Ensure that all activities in the classroom and larger school environment are linguistically and culturally responsive.
- Work with students to make transparent how language works (various forms for varied purposes).
- Offer students appropriate language support to engage in learning using academic language, and to engage in school-based performances.
- Create clear channels of communication with parents.
- Connect families to the academic practices of school.
- Ensure that all students have sufficient resources to carry out learning activities.

In these ways, classrooms and schools begin to be more equitable places, enabling all students to have access to learning. While other approaches identify specific ways in which languages may be taught and learned, a socio-cultural approach offers a possibility of equal access and participation for all students in schools.

Points for reflection

1 What 'forms of language' do your students need to know and use, across the range of subject areas, tasks and activities in your classroom, to be success-ful in school?
2 What, other than language itself, do successful performances entail in your context?
3 What participation patterns (whole group, small group work, pair work, one-on-one) do you utilize in your classroom? How do you decide which to use and when, and how do you evaluate effectiveness?
4 How do you connect with the families of students in your classroom in ways that enable you to learn from them?
5 How do you know what knowledge and experiences your (individual) students bring to school? How do you use those to shape your curriculum and instruction?

Suggestions for further reading

Gee, J. P. (1996) *Social Linguistics and Literacies: Ideology in Discourses*. Bristol, PA: Taylor and Francis.
Gonzalez, N., Moll, L. C. and Amanti, C. (2005) *Funds of Knowledge: Theorizing Practices in Households, Communities, and Classrooms*. Mahwah, NJ: Lawrence Erlbaum Associates.
Hawkins, M. R. (2004) 'Researching English language and literacy development in schools', *Educational Researcher*, 33 (3): 14–25.
Toohey, K. (2000) *Learning English at School: Identity, Social Relations and Classroom Practice*. Clevedon: Multilingual Matters.
Valdes, G. (1996) *Con Respeto: Bridging the Distance Between Culturally Diverse Families and Schools*. New York: Teachers College Press.

References

Gonzalez, N., Moll, L. C. and Amanti, C. (2005) *Funds of Knowledge: Theorizing Practices in Households, Communities and Classrooms*. Mahwah, NJ: Lawrence Erlbaum Associates.

Hawkins, M. and Nicoletti, K. (2008) 'Unpacking the science fair: Sociocultural approaches to teaching English-language learners', in C. Compton-Lilly (ed.), *Breaking the Silence: Recognizing and Valuing the Social and Cultural Knowledges of Children*. Newark, DE: International Reading Association.

Hawkins, M. R. (2005) 'Becoming a student: Identity work and academic literacies in early schooling', *TESOL Quarterly*, 39 (1): 59–80.

Heath, S. B. (1982) 'What no bedtime story means: Narrative skills at home and at school', *Language in Society*, 11 (2): 49–76.

Heath, S. B. (1983) *Ways With Words: Language, Life and Work in Communities and Classrooms*. Cambridge: Cambridge University Press.

Lave, J. and Wenger, E. (1991) *Situated Learning: Legitimate Peripheral Participation*. Cambridge: Cambridge University Press.

Rogoff, B. (1990) *Apprenticeship in Thinking: Cognitive Development in Social Context*. New York: Oxford University Press.

Tharp, R. G. and Yamauchi, L. A. (1994) *Effective Instructional Conversation in Native American Classrooms*, Educational Practice Report 10. NCRCDSLL Publications. www.ncela.gwu.edu/pubs/ncrcdsll/index.htm, accessed 15 September 2008.

Toohey, K. (2000) *Learning English at School: Identity, Social Relations and Classroom Practice*. Clevedon: Multilingual Matters.

Valdes, G. (2001) *Learning and Not Learning English: Latino Students in American Schools*. New York: Teachers College Press.

Vygotsky, L. S. 1(978) *Mind and Society.* Cambridge, MA: Harvard University Press.

8

Bilingual Approaches

Ester J. de Jong and

Rebecca Freeman Field

Traditionally, much debate about the schooling of bilingual learners in English-dominant countries has centred on the choice of medium of instruction: should students classified as English as an additional language (EAL) learners be taught exclusively in English or through a bilingual approach? While this debate might inform national policies to some limited extent, it has done little to improve our understanding of how classrooms and schools can be organized so that bilingual learners achieve academically, develop expertise in more than one language, and integrate into the classroom, school and community. For that, we need to move away from the quest for the best model to a set of principles that underlie quality schooling for all bilingual learners (Brisk, 2006), and select approaches that are realistic for our particular teaching and learning contexts.

We use the term 'bilingual learner' in this chapter to refer to students who are developing competence in more than one language, and we focus on contexts in which English is the dominant societal or 'majority' language. More specifically, bilingual learners include (1) students categorized by schools as EAL; (2) heritage language speakers who speak English and a home or heritage language other than English; and (3) English speakers who come from monolingual homes and are becoming bilingual at school. In English-dominant societies, EAL students and heritage language speakers are often referred to as 'minority language' speakers, reflecting power relations among languages and speakers of languages in that society.

We begin this chapter with three principles that educators can use to achieve their goals for bilingual learners. Quality schooling for bilingual learners (1) affirms linguistic and cultural identities, (2) promotes additive bilingualism, and (3) fosters integration. These principles stem from a fundamental pedagogical assumption and a commitment to social justice: in order to create optimal learning environments for bilingual learners, educators must build on what students already know, and we must do so equitably. The chapter then reviews a range of bilingual approaches that reflect these principles in different ways, from full-fledged bilingual education programs to heritage language classes to bilingual practices in English-medium classrooms. We highlight some of the challenges in implementing these three principles and conclude with a call to action on the local level that rejects the subordinate status of bilingual learners and the languages they speak, and that strives to provide access to equitable education for all.

A principled approach for bilingual learners

Principle 1: Quality schooling for bilingual learners affirms identities.

This first principle assumes that social identity construction is a fundamental aspect of schooling, and that teachers and learners play active roles in this process. Through their ongoing participation in language-mediated activities at school, teachers and students (co-)construct communities of practice and multiple identities within those communities (Freeman, 1998; Ochs and Schieffelin, 2008). The choices that educators make in organizing their programmes and practices have implications for the identity options available to bilingual learners.

Affirming identities of bilingual learners at school means that educators value the linguistic and cultural diversity in their classes, and draw on the linguistic and cultural resources, or 'funds of knowledge' (Moll, 1992), that learners bring with them to school to support and scaffold their learning. This principle requires educators to treat bilingual learners as complete individuals who are in the process of becoming bilingual and bicultural (or multilingual and multicultural), and not as deficient individuals because they don't speak English. Denying students' linguistic and cultural identities renders multilingual students invisible and inaudible, can limit their participation opportunities, and is associated with lower academic achievement (Cummins, 2001; García, 2008). Affirming the linguistic and cultural identities of bilingual learners can increase engagement with literacy activities and encourage investment in school (Cummins, 2006).

Principle 2: Quality schooling for bilingual learners promotes additive bilingualism.

This second principle reflects our language-as-resource orientation (Ruíz, 1984), and views the development of bilingualism (biliteracy, multilingualism, multilingual literacies) as an important goal and desirable outcome of schooling. Like Hornberger (2003) and García (2008), we see bilingual learners as situated within a continuum of bilingual and biliteracy (or multilingual and multilingual literacy) development. We know that bilingual learners can develop the ability to use multiple languages with varying degrees of expertise for different purposes over time.

The distinction between additive and subtractive bilingualism is important here, and is relevant not only to a discussion of bilingual education programmes but also to English-medium programmes. Additive bilingual programmes encourage learners to add a second, third, or fourth language to the students' existing linguistic repertoires. In contrast, subtractive programmes have no goal of first language (L1) maintenance or development. As students acquire English in these programmes, they tend to lose their L1 until they become dominant or even monolingual in English. Syntheses of empirical research demonstrate that a strong predictor of L2 literacy development is L1 literacy, and that additive bilingualism is associated with higher academic achievement than subtractive bilingualism (Genesee et al., 2007).

We recognize that not all schools can promote bilingualism and biliteracy to the same degree. In many contexts, additive bilingual education programmes simply are not possible. However, an additive bilingual *stance* is always possible and desirable from a social justice perspective because it aims to validate the linguistic (and cultural) resources of students and their families. Even in English-medium classrooms, teachers can use bilingual strategies to support the multiple languages and literacies of their students and communities.

Principle 3: Quality schooling for bilingual learners fosters integration.

This third principle recognizes that responses to linguistic and cultural diversity in schools are embedded in a wider sociopolitical context that affects decision-making processes and outcomes at the classroom, school and community levels. In its broadest sense, integration refers to bringing together different parts, on an equal basis, to make a whole (Brisk, 1991). When applied to schools, we see integration as a negotiated process that involves all participants, not only EAL students and their teachers. Everyone in the school is positioned as a full participant, and everyone learns to negotiate effectively in linguistically and culturally diverse situations. Thus, newcomers are provided with opportunities to learn the norms of interaction and interpretation guiding behaviour in their new school, and established community members (that is, educators, students) have opportunities to interact with and learn about these newcomers without stigmatizing their culturally shaped ways of thinking, being, valuing and interacting. In integrated communities, linguistic and cultural diversity strengthens, not threatens, the whole.

Integration is fostered equitably when the needs of all students, including those of bilingual learners, are an integral part of the school's organizational structure and decision-making processes. All educators who work with bilingual learners need to understand how these students learn in and through two languages at school. Decisions about curriculum content and materials, instruction, assessment, programme design, professional development, structuring of classroom interactions, extracurricular activities, and parental and community involvement all affect how linguistic and cultural diversity is integrated into the fabric of the school. When bilingual learners' strengths and needs are central, and not an afterthought, in such educational decision-making, bilingual learners can achieve.

These three principles (affirming linguistic and cultural identities, promoting additive bilingualism, and fostering integration) are grounded in research on quality schooling of bilingual learners, and reflect our understanding that bilingualism benefits the individual, local community, and larger society for cognitive, linguistic, sociocultural, political and economic reasons (Freeman, 2004). Each principle emphasizes slightly different aspects of the set of complex decisions that educators make about and through language. While neither principle is superior to the other, there are natural tensions in the implementation process among the three principles. For example, many programmes for bilingual learners segregate these students to promote their language and literacy development and to better meet their needs. However, this segregation can also unintentionally stigmatize bilingual learners and impede social integration. Educators need to balance attention to all three principles as they make decisions about schooling for their bilingual learners, and think creatively about ways they can address any imbalances they find.

Principles in practice

Quality schools for bilingual learners address all three principles; however, the choices that educators make will vary according to their community context, available resources (materials, qualified teachers), and their specific student populations. This section reviews a continuum of bilingual possibilities, from fully-fledged additive bilingual programmes to heritage language classes to bilingual practices within the context of English-medium classrooms. The ability of schools to develop extended bilingual repertoires for bilingual learners diminishes as (minority) languages are used for less time and for fewer purposes within the school and the community. By considering these approaches as a continuum we highlight the role of teachers as language planners and agents of change as they make decisions that are appropriate for their context.

Additive bilingual and multilingual programme models

Bilingual education by definition means using two languages for instructional purposes, typically the students' native language (L1) and a partner language (L2). In some cases, third (L3) or even fourth (L4) languages are added later in the programme, making it a multilingual programme. Additive bilingual environments can be created formally in schools through the implementation of specific language programmes that aim to develop competence in more than one language. Common additive bilingual and multilingual programme models can be distinguished by their language planning goals, target populations, and the ways that they distribute languages for instructional purposes. By design, these models aim for high levels of bilingual or multilingual competence and are the result of language policies that formally articulate specific learning environments for each of the languages, including how much time each language is used, what subjects in which language, and what languages at which grade levels.

Maintenance bilingual education: These programmes target minority language speakers (immigrant, indigenous, regional minority), and often aim to revitalize indigenous or regional minority languages in decline. Maintenance bilingual programmes generally include a strong focus on affirming identities, and they segregate minority language speakers from the majority language population for much or all of the bilingual learner's day. Research on these programmes demonstrates that they can be highly effective for minority language speakers (May, 2008).

Bilingual programmes for the deaf: These programmes exclusively target deaf students, and they teach content through sign language and the written form of the societal language. Deaf culture and identity is an important component of the bilingual programme to counter deficit views of individuals who are deaf or hard of hearing (Allen, 2002; LaSasso and Lollis, 2003; Skelton and Valentine, 2003).

Immersion: These programmes target majority language speakers (for example Anglophones in Canada) who receive most or all of their content area instruction, including initial literacy instruction, through the minority language (in this case, French). We find full or partial immersion programmes that vary in terms of how much content area instruction is provided in the minority language. Research demonstrates that these programmes can be highly effective for language majority students in terms of academic achievement, bilingualism and biliteracy development, and attitudes toward minority language speakers (Genesee, 2004).

Two-way immersion (TWI): These programmes target majority and minority language speakers who are integrated together for most or all of their content-area instruction through two languages. TWI programmes have three goals for their students: academic achievement in two languages, bilingualism and biliteracy development, and cross-cultural competence for all students, and they combine the best of maintenance bilingual education for language minority speakers and immersion education for majority language speakers. Research demonstrates that well-implemented TWI programmes are very effective (Howard, Sugarman, and Christian, 2003; Lindholm-Leary, 2001; see also www.cal.org for directory of TWI programmes in the US).

Mainstream Bilingual and Multilingual education models: Mainstream multilingual and bilingual models aim for multilingualism for majority language speakers. An example of mainstream bilingual education is the International Schools, mostly private schools that offer a full curriculum through two languages. Typically, these schools cater to the children from business people, government officials or other international sojourners (European Council of International Schools, 1998, cited in de Mejia, 2002), although local families increasingly enroll their children in these schools as well. The curriculum is often equally divided between the two languages and tends to follow the curriculum of the 'home country', e.g., French is taught using the national curriculum from France.

Another well-known example is the European school model. The European schools were originally designed for children of parents who worked for the European Coal and Steel Community and could be considered a multilingual variant of mainstream bilingual education (see below). There are now 12 European schools in Luxembourg, Belgium, Germany, Italy, the Netherlands and the UK, primarily enrolling the children of civil servants working for the European Union. The schools follow a common model with the goals of maintaining and developing the students' native language and cultural identity, developing proficiency in multiple other languages, and promoting a European identity (Beardsmore, 1995; Muller and Beardsmore, 2004).

Luxembourg has trilingual education for all students enrolled in the school system. Mandatory preschool education begins in Luxembourgish and this language continues as a language of instruction and as a subject throughout elementary school. German is introduced as a subject in the first year of primary school and then intensifies as a subject and medium of instruction until 6th grade. French is introduced as a subject in 2nd grade and then increases its role in the curriculum to be the exclusive medium of instruction by the age of 15. Foreign language education is introduced at the secondary level as well, including English, Latin, Spanish, Italian, or Greek (Hoffman, 1998).

Table 8.1 provides a summary of the models described above. It is important to note that most bilingual education programmes are strands within a school and not implemented school-wide. To promote the goals of additive bilingualism and integration, the entire school environment must support the programme. An isolated bilingual programme for minority language speakers that is assigned a low status within the school will be challenged to provide an additive and affirming learning environment for the bilingual learners it serves. In these cases, educators must consider how school-wide policies and practices affect the specialized programme (Brisk, 2006; Carter and Chatfield, 1986; de Jong, 1996). A commitment to the principles of quality schooling for bilingual learners requires educators to look beyond the choice of programme model to the larger sociolinguistic situation at school.

Table 8.1   Additive bilingual and multilingual programme models

Programme label	Language goals	Target population	Language use and distribution
Maintenance bilingual education	Bilingualism	Minority	First and second language
Bilingual education for the deaf	Bilingualism	Minority	First and second language
Immersion	Bilingualism	Majority	First and second language
Two-way immersion (TWI)	Bilingualism	Minority and majority	First and second language
Mainstream bilingual and multilingual education	Multilingualism	Minority, majority	First and second language, and third language (and optional fourth language)

(Sources: Baker, 2006; Brisk, 2006)

Heritage language classes

Unlike bilingual programmes where students learn in and through two languages, heritage language classes more resemble foreign language or language arts classes. These enrichment classes target heritage language speakers who may or may not be designated EAL, and aim to broaden their linguistic repertoires, generally with a focus on the standard language and literacy development in that language. Since the 1990s, we have seen growing interest in these classes/programmes in the United States, especially Spanish for native speakers (SNS) classes that are offered as part of the general education curriculum for credit (Roca and Colombí, 2003; Valdés, 2000).

Heritage language programmes are diverse in nature as schools and communities respond creatively to the resources and constraints (time, money, materials, personnel) in their local contexts. Examples include before- or after-school clubs or groups, heritage language classes for heritage language speakers, as well as classes for both English-speaking heritage language speakers and EAL students who speak the same language. At one international school in Vienna, educators recruited parent-volunteers to teach in their after-school 'mother tongue' programme, and their well-organized programme included classes in more than ten languages (Carder, personal communication). Other countries explore the option of integrating minority languages into the secondary 'foreign language' curriculum (Clyne et al., 2004). In an effort to legitimate these programmes and offer more options for bilingual learners, heritage language classes are often formally linked with Advance Placement (AP) classes or the International Baccalaureate (IB) programme.

While not within the confines of formal schooling, it is also worth mentioning the community-based language schools (Blackledge and Creese, 2008; Conteh et al., 2007; Creese et al., 2008). These are after-school programmes and Saturday schools that provide instruction in the students' heritage languages and cultures and are organized by the local community. Advocates for these programmes often look for linkages between formal schools and these community-run classes (Strand, 2007; Wei, 2006). For example, in one state in the United States (Connecticut) educators recently urged state law-makers to pass a law that allows students who attend heritage language schools and pass a language proficiency test to earn up to four elective credits towards fulfilling the state's high school graduation requirement or credit specifically towards a foreign language requirement (Vu, 2008). These kinds of school–community collaborations can support the development of multilingual repertoires and identities (Peyton et al., 2001).

Heritage language classes/programmes can address some of the challenges that schools face when they are working to promote additive bilingualism but cannot have a school-wide additive bilingual programme. While often limited in scope due to the limited amount of time students attend these classes, they can provide an important linguistic counterweight to the predominantly English instruction in school for minority language speakers.

Using bilingual teaching strategies

In some contexts, neither a fully developed bilingual programme nor a heritage language programme are possible ways to develop multilingual competence. Under these conditions, teachers' linguistic choices can still value and affirm the language resources that students and parents bring to school (Cummins, 2001). Effective teachers of bilingual learners draw on available language resources and use bilingual teaching strategies (Freeman and Freeman, 2000; Jacobson and Faltis, 1990; Lucas and Katz, 1994; Tikunoff and Vazquez-Faria, 1983). A few examples illustrate different ways students' first languages can be used strategically in any context.

Freeman and Freeman (2000) recommend the 'preview–view–review' strategy to teach complex content-area concepts to bilingual learners. Key concepts are introduced in the students' first language (preview), students work with those concepts in English (view), and then students review those concepts in their first language. The preview and review portions of the activity/lesson/thematic unit could be facilitated by the bilingual teacher, teaching assistant or tutor. Teachers can also structure the preview activities so that the bilingual learner works with a more competent bilingual peer to negotiate the meaning of that content area concept in their first language. The preview can be negotiated orally and/or it can draw on texts written in the L1; these L1 texts might be commercially made, teacher-made, student-made, or found on the internet. For example, a unit on matter may first elicit from students oral discussion of their experiences with liquids, solids and gas in their L1. During the view phase, the teacher can structure activities in which bilingual learners are integrated with English-speaking peers and use English to negotiate the meaning of the academic content that they were learning about in segregated L1 groups. In the case of a unit on matter, the teacher may ask students to conduct experiments and write down their observations in English, using writing scaffolds for beginning writers. For the review phase, teachers group bilingual learners together again to reinforce and extend their learning in their L1. In our example, the teacher could ask students to share their understandings of what matter is, forms of matter, and how matter changes, in their L1. This strategic, well-planned activity structure can simultaneously address the principles of affirming identities, promoting bilingualism, and fostering integration, and it can be used in English-medium and bilingual education contexts by monolingual or bilingual teachers.

To engage bilingual learners in a wide range of literacy activities that draw on the linguistic and cultural resources learners bring to school, Cummins (2006) recommends that teachers have students write dual language books or what he calls 'identity texts'. He describes a multilingual literacies project implemented by monolingual English-speaking teachers working in linguistically and culturally diverse English-medium schools in Toronto, Canada. These teachers invite their students to write about topics that are aligned with the regular content-area instruction, but written in English and their heritage language. Teachers organize students into same-language groups (bilingual Urdu/English speakers in one group, bilingual Bengali/English speakers in another group, for example), and students draw on each other's diverse language and literacy strengths in English and their heritage language to write their books in two languages. Students publish their dual language books in hard copy and on the web, which develops a multilingual library of student-made books for the school, facilitates students' development of computer literacies, and allows the books to reach a wider audience. (Go to http://thornwood.peelschools.org/Dual/ for a detailed description of this process and examples of student-made dual language books in a variety of languages.)

Other bilingual strategies that can be used in the English-medium classroom include the use of the native language for vocabulary development and/or concept clarification, for brainstorming or drafting, and assessment. Teachers can draw on the L1 to scaffold for explicit transfer across languages. Code-switching is another strategy that bilingual teachers employ to engage bilingual learners and make them feel an integral part of the classroom community (August et al., 2005; Cummins, 2005). Such code-switching does not imply simultaneous translation. Rather, teachers can use the native language to make students feel comfortable in the classroom (Lin, 2006). De Mejia (1998), for example, found that when a preschool teacher decided to include Spanish, in addition to English, in her story-telling, her native Spanish-speaking students were better able to contribute their ideas and actively participate in constructing meaning from the story. By using bilingual strategies, teachers can informally check for comprehension and allow students to demonstrate their knowledge through more than just one medium.

As illustrated, bilingual practices should not and do not have to be limited to bilingual teachers or bilingual classrooms. In addition to the strategies illustrated above, monolingual teachers can advocate for native language tutors, acquire native language materials for their classroom, learn some basic phrases in their students' native language, ask their students to share and teach their languages, and create opportunities for students to use their native languages with each other socially as well as for academic learning (Gravelle, 1996; Irujo, 1998).

An approach to teaching bilingual learners that is grounded in the principles of affirming identities, promoting additive bilingualism, and fostering integration has the advantage that it applies across many learning contexts with multilingual learners. Although the implementation of a programme model that supports multilingual competence is preferable, schools that cannot implement such a programme can still organize their policies and practices around these principles in order to optimize learning environments for all learners. The three principles focus educators' attention on slightly different aspects of the complex decisions they make about and through language in their classrooms and in their school. Effective educators recognize and respond to the different paths that bilingual learners take depending on (a) where learners are situated on the continuum of bilingual and biliteracy development, and (b) their consideration of resources and constraints in the local context. Purposeful and principled language planning decisions can contribute to the development of a school environment where all students develop multilingual literacies to the greatest degree possible.

Taking it to your school

Effective educators for bilingual learners recognize the balancing act that is necessary to build a linguistically and culturally affirming, additive, integrated and equitable learning environment. For instance, TWI programmes often require teachers to adhere to a strict separation of languages. While this strategy supports the goal of equity in language use and exposure to target language models across a wide range of communicative contexts (Howard et al., 2003), it may also lead to missed opportunities for explicit teaching for cross-linguistic transfer and the development of metalinguistic awareness. When teachers see themselves as language planners, they critically analyse policies in relation to their students' strengths and needs, and they consider the extent to which the policy supports or hinders their classroom efforts to reach their language planning goals. When they see themselves as agents of change, they think systemically and strategically about the challenges they identify, and they collaborate with their colleagues to modify their approach in ways that are aligned with the principles of quality schooling for bilingual learners and appropriate for their context.

We conclude this chapter by encouraging educators, working in collaborative action-oriented professional learning communities (Dufour and Eaker, 1998), to investigate their general school environment, educational policies, programmes, curriculum content, materials, instruction, assessments, extracurricular activities, and home–school connections to see to what degree each of these aspects of decision-making reflects the principles of affirming linguistic and cultural identities, promoting additive bilingualism, and fostering integration. Questions such as the following could guide their inquiry:

- Are the languages of the bilingual learners at the school readily observable and audible in classrooms and throughout the school?
- Is there a language policy for the school, and does it include an additive bilingual stance?
- Do the curriculum content and classroom materials include the contributions and perspectives of the range of cultural groups represented at the school?
- Are classroom activities organized in ways that validate the norms of interaction and interpretation that students bring with them to school so that all students have opportunities to participate in the active construction of meaning?
- Are opportunities for engagement and learning distributed equitably across different language contexts within the classroom and the school?
- Do assessments reflect an additive bilingual stance that views students' abilities through both languages?
- Are the assessments used to demonstrate achievement valid for multilingual learners and do they yield reliable evidence of student growth over time?
- Are assessment results used to evaluate programme practices against programme goals and to make changes in curriculum and instructional approaches?

When teachers and administrators clearly understand how the principles of affirming identities, promoting bilingualism, and fostering integration are central to every level of decision-making, and when they see themselves as language planners and agents of change, they can create a school environment that enables all learners, including those who are bilingual, to participate and achieve. In this way, educators collectively reject the subordinate positioning of language minority students that we see in so many schools worldwide, and potentially transform social relations on the local level. When teachers identify the range of linguistic resources they can draw on, and broaden their notion of teaching and learning in ways that position bilingual learners, bilingual teaching assistants, and other bilingual family and community members as partners in the construction of knowledge in the classroom, all kinds of possibilities can emerge.

Points for reflection

1 What evidence can you find of ways that policies, programmes and practices at your school affirm students' linguistically and culturally diverse identities, promote additive bilingualism, and foster integration?
2 What evidence can you find of ways that policies, programmes and practices at your school deny students' linguistically and culturally diverse identities, lead to subtractive bilingualism, and marginalize language minority students?
3 What action steps can you take to build on the principles of quality schooling for bilingual learners in your classroom, school and community?

Suggestions for further reading

Fortune, T. W. and Tedick, D. J. (2008) *Pathways to Multilingualism: Evolving Perspectives on Immersion (Bilingual) Education and Bilingualism*. Clevedon: Multilingual Matters.
García, O. (2008). *Bilingual Education in the 21st Century: A Global Perspective*. Malden, MA: Wiley-Blackwell.
García, O., Skutnabb-Kangas, T. and Torres-Guzmán, E. (2006) *Imagining Multilingual Schools: Languages in Education and Glocalization*. Clevedon: Multilingual Matters.

References

Allen, B. M. (2002) 'ASL-English bilingual classroom: The families' perspectives', *Bilingual Research Journal,* 26: 1–20.
August, D., Carlo, M., Dressler, C. and Snow, C. E. (2005) 'The critical role of vocabulary development for English language learners', *Learning Disabilities Research & Practice,* 20 (1): 50–7.
Baker, C. (2006) *Foundations of Bilingual Education and Bilingualism*, 4th edn. Clevedon: Multilingual Matters.

Beardsmore, H. B. (1995) 'The European school experience in multilingual education', in T. Skutnabb-Kangas (ed.), *Multilingualism for All*. Lisse, Netherlands: Swets and Zeitlinger (pp. 21–68).

Blackledge, A. and Creese, A. (2008) 'Contesting "language" as "heritage": Negotiation of identities in late modernity', *Applied Linguistics*, 29 (4): 533–54.

Brisk, M. E. (1991). 'Toward multilingual and multicultural mainstream education', *Journal of Education,* 173 (2): 114–29.

Brisk, M. E. (2006) *Bilingual Education: From Compensatory to Quality Education*, 2nd edn. Mahwah, NJ: Lawrence Erlbaum Associates.

Carter, T. P. and Chatfield, M. (1986) 'Effective schools for language minority students', *American Journal of Education*, 97: 200–33.

Cenoz, J. (2005) 'English in bilingual programs in the Basque Country', *International Journal of the Sociology of Language*, 171: 41–56.

Clyne, M., Isaakidi, T., Liem, I. and Hunt, R. (2004) 'Developing and sharing community language resources through secondary school programmes', *International Journal of Bilingual Education and Bilingualism,* 7 (4): 255–78.

Conteh, J., Martin, P. and Robertson, L. H. (2007) *Multilingual Learning: Stories from Schools and Communities in Britain*. Stoke on Trent: Trentham Books.

Creese, A., Baraç, T., Bhatt, A., Blackledge, A., Hamid, S., Li Wei, Lytra, V., Martin, P., Wu, C.-J. and Ya cio lu-Ali, D. (2008) *Investigating Multilingualism in Complementary Schools in Four Communities,* Final Report, RES-000-23-1180. Birmingham: University of Birmingham.

Cummins, J. (2001) *Negotiating Identities: Education for Empowerment in a Diverse Society,* 2nd edn. Los Angeles, CA: California Association for Bilingual Education.

Cummins, J. (2005) 'A proposal for action: Strategies for recognizing heritage language competence as a learning resource within the mainstream classroom', *Modern Language Journal*, 89 (4): 585–92.

Cummins, J. (2006) 'Identity texts: The imaginative construction of self through multiliteracies pedagogy', in O. García, T. Skutnabb-Kangas and M. Torres-Guzmán (eds), *Imagining Multilingual Schools: Languages in Education and Glocalization*. Clevedon: Multilingual Matters (pp. 51–68).

de Jong, E. J. (1996) 'Integrating Language Minority Education in Elementary Schools', unpublished dissertation. Boston, MA: Boston University.

de Mejia, A.-M. (1998) 'Bilingual storytelling: Code switching, discouse control, and learning opportunities', *TESOL Journal* (Winter): 4–10.

Dufour, R. and Eaker, R. (1998) *Professional Learning Communities: Best Practices for Enhancing Student Achievement*. Bloomington, IN: National Education Service.

Freeman, R. (1998) *Bilingual Education and Social Change*. Clevedon: Multilingual Matters.

Freeman. R. (2004) *Building on Community Bilingualism*. Philadelphia, PA: Caslon.

Freeman, D. and Freeman, Y. (2000) *Teaching Reading in Multilingual Classrooms*. Portsmouth, NH: Heinemann.

García, O. (2008) 'Imagining Multilingual TESOL', symposium presented at National TESOL conference, New York.

Genesee, F. (2004) 'What do we know about bilingual education for majority language students?', in T. K. Bhatia and W. Ritchie (eds), *Handbook of Bilingualism and Multiculturalism*. Malden, MA: Blackwell (pp. 547–76).

Genesee, F., Lindholm-Leary, K., Saunders, W. and Christian, D. (2007) *Educating English Language Learners: A Synthesis of Empirical Evidence*. New York: Cambridge University Press.

Gorter, D. (2005) 'Three languages of instruction in Fryslan', *International Journal of the Sociology of Language*, 171: 57–73.

Gravelle, M. (1996) *Supporting Bilingual Learners in School*. Stoke-on-Trent: Trentham Books.

Hoffman, C. (1998) 'Luxembourg and the European Schools', in J. Cenoz and F. Genesee (eds), *Beyond Bilingualism: Multilingualism and Multilingual Education*. Clevedon: Multilingual Matters. (pp. 143–74).

Hornberger, N. (2003) *The Continua of Biliteracy*. Clevedon: Multilingual Matters.

Howard, E., Sugarman, J. and Christian, D. (2003) 'Trends in two-way immersion education: A review of the research', *Center for Research on the Education of Students placed at Risk (CRESPAR)*, Vol. 3. Baltimore, MD: Johns Hopkins University.

Irujo, S. (1998) *Teaching Bilingual Children: Beliefs and Behaviors*. Boston, MA: Heinle and Heinle.

Jacobson, R. and Faltis, C. J. (1990) *Language Distribution Issues in Bilingual Schooling*. Philadelphia, PA: Multilingual Matters.

LaSasso, C. and Lollis, J. (2003) 'Survey of residential and day schools for deaf students in the United States that identify themselves as bilingual-bicultural programs', *Journal of Deaf Studies and Deaf Education*, 8 (1): 79–91.

Lin, A. (2006) 'Beyond linguistic purism in language-in-education policy and practice: Exploring bilingual pedagogies in a Hong Kong science classroom', *Language and Education*, 20 (4): 287–305.

Lindholm-Leary, K. (2001) *Dual Language Education*. Clevedon: Multilingual Matters.

Lopez-Robertson, J. (2006) 'The making of a bilingual educator', *Language Arts*, 83 (5): 388–9.

Lucas, T. and Katz, A. (1994) 'Reframing the debate: The roles of native languages in English-only programs for language minority students', *TESOL Quarterly*, 28 (3).

May, S. (2008) 'Bilingual/immersion education: What the research tells us', in J. Cummins and N. Hornberger (eds), *Encyclopedia of Language and Education*, 2nd edn, Vol. 5: Bilingual Education. New York: Springer Science/Business Media LLC. (pp. 19–34).

Moll, L. (1992) 'Bilingual classrooms and community analysis: Some recent trends', *Educational Researchers*, 21 (2): 20–4.

Muller, A. and Beardsmore, H. B. (2004) 'Multilingual interaction in plurilingual classes – European school practice', *International Journal of Bilingual Education and Bilingualism*, 7 (1): 24–42.

Ochs, E. and Schieffelin, B. (2008) 'Language socialization: An historical overview', in P. A. Duff and N. H. Hornberger (eds), *Encyclopedia of Language and Education*, 2nd edn, Vol. 8: Language Socialization. New York: Springer Science/Business Media LLC. (pp. 3–15).

Peyton, J., Ranard, D. and McGinnis, S. (2001) *Heritage Languages in America: Preserving a National Resource*. McHenry, IL: Delta Systems Co.

Roca, A. and Colombí, M. (2003) *Mi Lengua: Spanish as a Heritage Language in the United States*. Washington, DC: Georgetown University Press.

Ruíz, R. (1984) 'Orientations in language planning', *NABE Journal*, 8 (2): 15–34.

Skelton, T. and Valentine, G. (2003) ' "It feels like being Deaf is normal": an exploration into the complexities of defining D/deafness and young D/deaf people's identities', *Canadian Geographer*, 47 (4): 451–66.

Strand, S. (2007) 'Surveying the views of pupils attending supplementary schools in England', *Educational Research*, 49 (1): 1–19.

Tikunoff, W. J. and Vazquez-Faria, J. A. (1983) 'Successful schooling for bilingual children', *Peabody Journal of Education*, 59 (4): 234–71.

Valdés, G. (2000) 'Introduction', *Spanish for Native Speakers: AATSP Professional Development Series Handbook for Teachers K-16*. Orlando, FL: Harcourt College.

Vu, P. (2008) *States Credit Foreign Language Study*. www.stateline.org/live/details/story?contentId=320478a, accessed 28 July 2008.

Wei, L. (2006) 'Complementary schools, past, present and future', *Language and Education*, 20 (1): 76–83.

Concluding Remarks
Constant Leung and
Angela Creese

The eight substantive chapters in this collection have provided glimpses of the complex conceptual, linguistic, sociocultural and ideological issues in the education for students from diverse language backgrounds within our schooling systems. The contributing authors have tried to examine these issues from both bottom-up and top-down perspectives. Manny Vazquez and Alan Williams, for instance, find aspects of their routinized curriculum and classroom practices problematic for some of their students, and proceed to provide an analysis and pedagogic response with reference to additional and complementary principles drawing on relevant research and theories. Others, for example Candace Harper and her colleagues, begin with a reflexive examination of aspects of the prevailing curriculum principles in their working contexts. They then consider the merits of alternative and/or complementary approaches with reference to classroom practice.

In one way or another, the stances taken up by the contributing authors of these accounts reflect what Kumaravadivelu (2003) would refer to as the 'postmethod condition'. That is, these practitioners–researchers, *qua* authors, have tried to analyse and reflect on their experience and work to respond to the language education needs of students in a local context, and to construct personal theories of practice (also see Introduction). This is entirely consistent with what we now know about teacher thinking and teacher practice. Historically speaking, one conventional view of teachers is that they are educational professionals who help students to learn particular bodies of knowledge by implementing certain classroom processes. On this view teachers can be trained to follow pedagogic procedures, and their professional practice is essentially guided by a prevailing curriculum regime. Research in teacher cognition and practice in the past 20 years or so has shown that this 'teacher as operator' view is far too simplistic. Increasingly it is understood that teachers rarely *implement* teaching theories and classroom procedures handed down to them on teacher education and professional development courses in any straightforward way. Johnson (2006: 236) puts it succinctly: 'teachers' prior experiences, their interpretations of the activities they engage in, and, most important, the contexts within which they work are extremely influential in shaping how and why teachers do what they do'. There is very little evidence that teachers simply follow teaching approaches and methods given to them on training courses or in curriculum prescriptions in a mechanical fashion in their teaching. Concepts, principles and theories are mediated by teachers' perceptions of their pedagogic aims and their understanding of what counts as appropriate and workable in their local contexts; all of this is framed within teachers' personal biography, intellectual leanings and wider social and ideological values and commitments. We will return to this point on teachers as persons with values and agency in a moment.

Before we do that, we first look at Ivanič's (2004) analysis of teachers' perspectives on the teaching of writing in English as an illustration of teachers' divergent professional orientations and dispositions. Although the specific teachers involved in the study were working with adult students, the findings are relevant to the point under discussion; that is, that teachers have divergent views. By examining a large array of sources of information on the teaching of writing – policy documents, pedagogic materials, and interviews with teachers and learners – Ivanič found that there are six discourses or approaches to the teaching of writing, and they represent 'recognizable associations among values, beliefs and practices which lead to particular forms of situated action, to particular decisions, choices and omissions, as well as to particular wording' (Ivanič, 2004: 220). These approaches are glossed as follows:

- *Skills*. Teachers prioritize rules of language, for example sentence level grammar and spelling; accuracy in the application of grammar rules would be regarded as a sign of successful learning.
- *Creativity*. Teachers encourage students to use their own experience to produce text; the ability to create interesting content and style of writing is valued.
- *Process*. Teachers are interested in helping students to plan, draft and revise their writing systematically; evidence of student drafting and revising is regarded as highly desirable.
- *Genre*. Teachers foreground the importance of recognizing different text types for different social purposes (such as a job application letter, rules and regulations of a social club); helping students to use appropriate language to produce texts for different social purposes is an important part of their work.
- *Social practice*. Teachers regard writing as part of community participation; helping students to write in ways that are in practice in their communities underpins this view of teaching.
- *Sociopolitical*. Teachers acknowledge that writing is implicated in social and political processes; explicit analysis of social and political power relation-ships and producing texts that can challenge existing power relations are important elements of teaching.

These approaches are related to very different intellectual and ideological traditions. One salient point for this discussion is that teachers associating themselves with, say, the process approach to the teaching of writing would likely respond to a curriculum based on a skills approach by making conceptual, epistemological and procedural adjustments in their teaching (if at all). And this is why it is important to consider teachers as persons with values and agency.

The term 'agency' is understood here to refer to the sum total of an individual's enactments of their needs, intentions, aspirations and desires in social action: 'a continuous flow of conduct' (Giddens, 1979: 54). Agency exists in relation to an individual's biography and intellectual dispositions within a particular cultural milieu. Here the concept of figured world proposed by Holland and her colleagues is particularly helpful. For individuals a figure world is, 'A socially and culturally constructed realm of interpretation in which particular characters and actors are recognised, significance is assigned to certain acts, and particular outcomes are valued over others' (Holland et al., 1998: 52).

When we talk about a person's moral compass, ambition or career drives, we are in effect referring to their thoughts and actions in relation to their figured world. If we see teachers' thinking and actions in these terms, then we can begin to understand that we should not expect teachers to act as compliant implementation operators of handed-down teaching approaches and methods. Teachers' understanding and use of any educational principle and pedagogy should be seen as 'socially situated and contingent on knowledge of self, students, subject matter, curricula' (Johnson, 2006: 239). And of course the situated and contingent nature of teachers' uptake (or not) of particular curriculum arrangements and pedagogic practices would depend on their values and ideological positions. This brings us to the final point: teacher professionalism.

Leung (2009) discusses two kinds of teacher professionalism: sponsored professionalism and independent professionalism. In an everyday sense teacher professionalism is often seen from an institutional perspective (such as university teacher education programmes) and/or from an official perspective (such as statutory qualificatory regulations). This kind of professionalism can be characterized and defined differently at different times and in different places by professional authorities and/or political agencies. All such instances of institutionally endorsed and publicly heralded definitions can be regarded as examples of sponsored professionalism. This kind of professionalism is usually proclaimed on behalf of and imposed upon teachers en masse; therefore it does not necessarily coincide with individual teachers' views on their work or their aspirations. It is generally an embodiment of a particular set of valued knowledge and ideology. For instance, some education systems would espouse the virtues of formal grammar teaching in English (or any language) and a transmission-based classroom pedagogy; others would prefer a more language-as-personal-expression approach to language teaching and a dialogic classroom practice. To achieve this kind of professionalism teachers will minimally need to obtain the qualified status required by monitoring or watchdog authorities. Furthermore, teachers may also need to meet the expectations of the prevailing education policies and curriculum regimes. For instance, in the past few years schoolteachers working in the USA would need to show that they are compliant with the curriculum and assessment requirements laid down by the No Child Left Behind legislation. In the UK since the early 1990s schoolteachers have been required to work with the various versions of the National Curriculum and National Strategies. The important point to note is that sponsored professionalism is not a fixed phenomenon (although it infuses a teacher's work while it lasts); it changes over time alongside the wider changes in social and political policies, as the recent experiences in the USA and the UK would show.

If sponsored collective professionalism represents a particular view of education (in its broadest sense), which may or may not be responsive to some fundamental and/or emergent issues in a rapidly changing social world, and if as teachers we wish to adopt an enquiring and sceptical (but not necessarily hostile) stance on handed-down theories and principles, then there is a need for teachers to be engaged in reflexive examination of their own beliefs and action. Reflexivity is the capacity and willingness to turn our thinking and action on themselves, and in so doing make them an object available for self-examination (Babcock, 1980; also see Johnson, 2000). By independent professionalism is meant a commitment to reflexive and critical examination of the educational values, pedagogic assumptions, knowledge bases and curriculum practices built into sponsored professionalism, and to take initiative and action to open up debates and to effect change where appropriate. Of course, this kind of professionalism presupposes a commitment to rendering one's own value basis explicit and to making conscious choices – professionally to comply with sponsored models and/or regulatory stipulations (and the associated values), or to engage in open discussion on their educational, pedagogic and social validity, and to promote alternative and/or complementary development where necessary. This book, we hope, has made a modest contribution to the latter.

References

Babcock, B. (1980) 'Reflexivity: definitions and discriminations', *Semiotica*, 30 (1/2): 1–14.

Giddens, A. (1979) *Central Problems in Social Theory: Action, Structure and Contradiction in Social Analysis*. Berkeley, CA: University of California Press.

Holland, D., Lachiotte, J. W., Skinner, D. and Cain, C. (1998) *Identity and Agency in Cultural Worlds*. Cambridge, MA: Harvard University Press.

Ivanič, R. (2004) 'Discourses of writing and learning to write', *Language and Education*, 18 (3): 220–45.

Johnson, K. E. (2000) 'Innovations in TESOL teacher education: a quiet revolution', in K. E. Johnson (ed.), *Teacher Education*. Alexandria, VA: TESOL (pp. 1–7).

Johnson, K. E. (2006) 'The sociocultural turn and its challenges for second language teacher education', *TESOL Quarterly*, 40 (1): 235–57.

Kumaravadivelu, B. (2003) *Beyond Methods: Macrostrategies for Language Teaching*. New Haven, CT and London: Yale University Press.

Leung, C. (2009) 'Second language teacher professionalism', in J. Richards and A. Burns (eds), *Cambridge Guide to Second Language Teacher Education*. Cambridge: Cambridge University Press. (pp. 49–58).

Author Index

Subject Index

Exciting Early Years and Primary Texts from SAGE

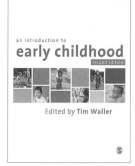

Exciting Education Texts from SAGE

School-based Research
A guide for education students
Elaine Wilson
978-1-4129-4850-0

TEACHING ENGLISH
CAROL EVANS
ALYSON MIDGLEY
PHIL RIGBY
LYNNE WARHAM
PETER WOOLNOUGH
978-1-4129-4818-0

Achieving your PTLLS Award
A Practical Guide to Successful Teaching in the Lifelong Learning Sector
Mary Francis
Jim Gould
978-1-84787-917-2

Introduction to Research Methods in Education
Keith F Punch
978-1-84787-018-6

A Toolkit for the effective Teaching Assistant
2nd Edition
Maureen Parker, Chris Lee, Stuart Gunn, Kitty Heardman, Rachael Hincks, Mary Pittman and Mark Townsend
978-1-84787-943-1

SECOND EDITION
GREG LIGHT, ROY COX and SUSANNA CALKINS
LEARNING and TEACHING in HIGHER EDUCATION
The REFLECTIVE PROFESSIONAL
978-1-84860-008-9

TEACHING SCIENCE
TONY LIVERSIDGE
MATT COCHRANE
BERNARD KERFOOT
JUDITH THOMAS
978-1-84787-362-0

The Complete Guide to Becoming an English Teacher Second Edition
Edited by Stephen Clarke, Paul Dickinson & Jo Westbrook
978-1-84787-289-0

3rd Edition
Daniel Muijs and David Reynolds
Effective Teaching
Evidence and Practice
978-1-84920-076-9

Find out more about these titles and our wide range of books for education students and practitioners at **www.sagepub.co.uk/education**